THE SEVERN VALLEY RAILWAY
A Past and Present Companion

SVR
•1970-2010•
40 YEARS OF STEAM

Past and
Present

Past & Present Publishing Ltd

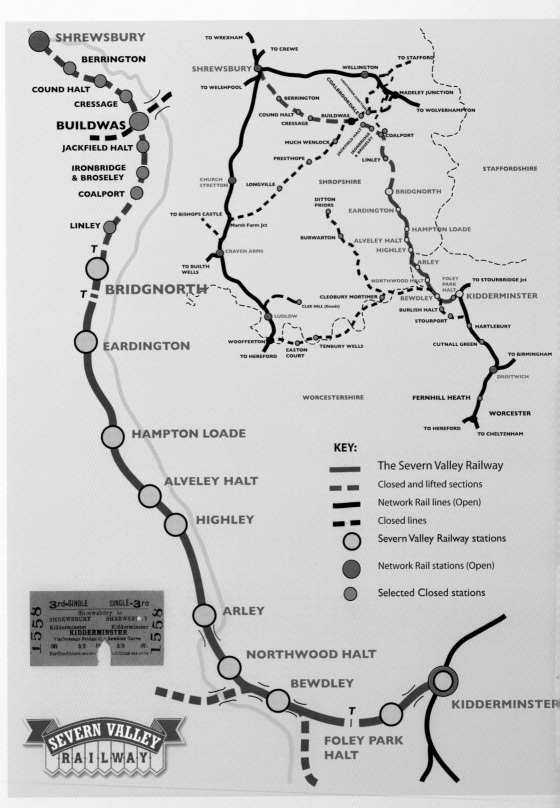

Map of the Severn Valley Railway and associated lines

THE SEVERN VALLEY RAILWAY
Volume 2

A PAST AND PRESENT COMPANION

Another nostalgic trip along the whole route from Kidderminster to Shrewsbury

John Stretton

Railway Heritage

from

The NOSTALGIA Collection

ISBN 978 1 85895 264 2

Past & Present Publishing Ltd
The Trundle
Ringstead Road
Great Addington
Kettering
Northants NN14 4BW

Tel/Fax: 01536 330588
email: sales@nostalgiacollection.com
Website: www.nostalgiacollection.com

Printed and bound in the Czech Republic

SVR
·1970-2010·
40 YEARS OF STEAM

First Edition published 23 May 2010

British Library Cataloguing in Publication Data
A catalogue record for this book is available from
the British Library.

Title page 'Past and present' in one image, as ex-LNWR No 3020 *Cornwall* receives due attention while on display in Bridgnorth's platform in August 1979. Though the ancient locomotive is certainly an eye-catching exhibit, it will not be moving anywhere fast, as evidenced by the blocks under the rear engine wheel and string tied around the cylinder! Built at Crewe as a 4-2-2 in 1847 for the Grand Junction Railway (later to become part of the LNWR), to a design of Richard Trevithick, it was rebuilt as a 2-2-2 in 1858; the name was in honour of his home county. Once housed at The Railway Age in Crewe, it has now been an incumbent of the NRM at York for many years. *Peter Johnson*

ACKNOWLEDGEMENTS

As usual, I am indebted to a wide variety and number of people who have assisted in one way or another. Photographers, especially, have been very willing to submit their images for consideration and I am truly grateful to those who aided in this way – without them and their foresight in pointing the camera at strategic moments the book would have struggled to be born! They are duly credited throughout the collection, but I take this opportunity to offer all of them my profound gratitude. In addition, there are those who have helped me before and have been fool enough to put their name in the frame again! Amongst all of these, there are some who deserve especial mention and I would like to here present my sincere thanks to Ben Ashworth, Edwin Wilmshurst, Richard Casserley, Paul Chancellor, Robin Leleux, Bryan Hicks, Laurence Waters and Michael Mensing. Aside from photographers, I would like to acknowledge the assistance and cooperation of: Dewi Jones (for his understanding and cooperation), the various signalmen to whom I spoke, Shu-Ju Lee, Dominic Jones, the 'guys' at Coalport, Pauline Hannigan (for her knowledge, time and car at Jackfield!) and Gary Thornton. Finally, as usual, thanks go to all at Silver Link – Peter for encouragement and for putting up with countless phone calls, and David for his unflinching patience and courtesy. Thank you all! The illustrations credited 'MJS' are mine.

CONTENTS

Prior to the preservation era, Kidderminster had enjoyed two shed sites. The initial facility opened in September 1852, on the east of the main line through the town, immediately to the south of the station. A one-road, dead-end affair, it was complete with coal stage and a 42-foot turntable. In 1899 the turntable was removed and the shed made a through type. Closed in 1932, a corrugated-iron, two-road, dead-end alternative was provided a little further south, in the 'V' between the main line and the Severn Valley line, otherwise known as the 'Kidderminster Loop'. On 10 September 1949 this second shed is the temporary resting place for Manning Wardle 0-6-0PT No 29 of the former Cleobury Mortimer & Ditton Priors Railway – built as a saddle-tank and sometime named *Cleobury*. Rebuilt as a pannier tank in 1924, it was later fitted with this delightful and literally arresting chimney! *H. C. Casserley*

INTRODUCTION

As owners of my previous 'Past and Present' books will know, I derive much pleasure in their production, especially in this 'Companion' series. There are various stages before completion and all have their own delights, but preparing a second volume of a book is both easier and harder than the first outing! This latest is a mixture of both, but I am happy to say that the delights and satisfactions far outweigh whatever negatives there may be (and I am not talking photography here!). A common theme with previous offerings

The topography of the Severn Valley Railway is constantly undulating, for the whole length from Kidderminster to Bridgnorth, and even the relatively short 'Kidderminster Loop' section has its distinct features. One such is Foley Park Tunnel, from which No 80079 bursts on 17 April 1977 on its way to Bewdley. Note the largely clear surroundings, both above the tunnel and on either side of the line; this is no longer the case, with dramatic growth over the ensuing three decades. New from Brighton Works in 1954, the 'Standard 4' tank moved to Barry Docks for scrapping in 1966 after withdrawal from BR but, happily, was saved for posterity, on the fledgling SVR, in 1971. *Tom Heavyside*

has been the cooperation and support from the railways concerned – as it should be of course – but I have to say that I really could not have asked for more than that shown to me by the Severn Valley Railway (SVR). The access given to normally 'off-limits' areas was both appreciated and tremendously rewarding; and I was also blessed with several occasions of serendipity, when events, etc, turned out better than I had dared hope. To all concerned I hereby tender my sincere thanks and gratitude – they have made the putting together of words and pictures a delight. I hope the reader shares the enjoyment. As those who know me will be aware, I do not like reusing images previously included in publications but, in this collection, I make no excuses for revisiting one or two images, and the reasons are mostly contained in the relevant captions. I hope readers will understand and forgive me!

Much has happened over the years since the first volume hit the bookstalls, not least of course the 2007 flooding and the construction of The Engine House. I felt that these deserved especial attention and they are given sections of their own at the end of the book. For the images for these and his ready assistance and cooperation, I am greatly indebted to Dewi Jones, Traffic Manager of the railway. His help is emblematic of what I referred to in the first paragraph and he, his courtesy and his humanity are a credit to the SVR.

Although the railway achieved its full length, from Bridgnorth to Kidderminster, in 1984, this has not stopped progress and development. No business can stand still – it either goes forward or backward. Whether consciously or not, the railway has grasped this particular nettle and continues to provide much for the visiting public to enjoy and for which to make return visits. The Engine House at Highley, the roofing of the waiting area at Kidderminster, the erection of a footbridge at Highley (ongoing as this volume was in production), and the proposed £400,000 diesel shed at Kidderminster, are just four of many highlights, but behind the scenes there are many other concepts in train, such as the ongoing Driver Experience courses, the exploration of a commuter service between Bewdley and Kidderminster, and the first-ever direct run from

Bridgnorth to Marylebone on 15 August 2009, in conjunction with Chiltern Railways.

Mention of the terrible flooding in the summer of 2007 brings to mind how close the railway could have come to disaster and closure of much of the route. That it has overcome and more than just survived is credit to all concerned on the SVR, but also the support given to it by other railways, the general public and the various grant-awarding authorities. When one considers that just operating a 16-mile railway – the SVR is the second-longest private railway on the ex-GWR – with much volunteer input, is a huge undertaking, it almost beggars belief that it could survive the aftermath of damage – much very severe – at 45 locations! The £3.8 million cost of reopening the line between Bewdley and Bridgnorth – in just 274 days! – would have deterred less sturdy souls from even considering the possibilities, but they knuckled down, got on with the job and are still here to tell the tale and give us all great pleasure. They deserve to succeed for many years to come on this aspect alone. And the importance of the railway cannot be underestimated. Kidderminster, Bridgnorth and Bewdley, as the three major stops along the way, would all notice the difference if the railway was not there; and, as one example from 'beyond the fence', the owners of Stanmore Hall tourist park at Bridgnorth have commented that bookings have soared since the reopening of the line. This cloud has also had another silver lining, in that there has been a surge in membership – to almost 13,500 – in the aftermath of the publicity generated by the disaster. Such has been the affection for the railway throughout the UK and beyond.

As with my previous books, I have thoroughly enjoyed 'going back in time' – which is not always easy, with tree growth especially irksome at times, together with the difficulty in judging just where the original photographer was standing or, in the case of the dismantled line north of Bridgnorth, where that exact location was! Deep down I feel we all enjoy wallowing in nostalgia and I hope that you, dear reader, will equally enjoy this journey. The images have been carefully chosen and I hope you will excuse the occasional diversion from a strict 'past and present' comparison – some of the images deserve to be seen for their own merit alone. As I have said before, if anyone finds factual errors or would like to add to the well of knowledge plumbed for the book, or, indeed, would like to pass on any messages

It has been a truism throughout the preservation movement of the past 50 years that the presence, enthusiasm and skills of volunteers are vital to run, maintain and extend the various enterprises. Happily, it is not just men who want to 'play trains'! One fine example of the fairer sex is Jane Collins, here seen ready, complete with appropriate uniform and tools of the trade, to act as Guard on a train from Kidderminster on 15 October 1988. Where is she now, one wonders! *Bryan Hicks*

and/or comments about the collection, I would be pleased to hear from them via the publisher. Any errors are mine alone and I would like any to be corrected in time for any possible future reprint. Thank you.

We are fortunate that there were – and still are – skilful, dedicated and energetic photographers who thought nothing of travelling the length and breadth of the UK, capturing images on film. There are undoubtedly more views of the railways of the SVR 'out there' – and there have been far too many left out of this volume purely for reasons of space. Again, I would be delighted to hear of any, especially from photographers who have not had their work previously published. Finally, by all means use this book as a sort of travel guide go out and enjoy yourselves!

Above: Passengers arriving at Kidderminster in BR days were greeted by this delightful Mock Tudor station, seen on 5 August 1963. Sadly, the highly attractive black and white timber structure began to shows distinct signs of age into the 1960s, with dry rot especially threatening collapse and causing it to be demolished in 1968. A small brick replacement building was put in place as an emergency, with a view to an improvement at some later stage. A £2.5 million replacement for the 21st century was given approval in July 2009, with Network Rail and others considering a new facility in Great Western style, to harmonise with the Severn Valley's adjacent terminus. Note the separate Luggage Entrance, bus and train timetables and period vehicles.

Right: The cobbles remain, as do the road overbridge and the ramped accesses on either side of the tracks, but otherwise the view is very different. Ahead of any further design alterations to the station building, a new footbridge/lift facility – costing some £300,000 – was opened during 2009, as part of improved disability access, off the picture to the right. In this view from 12 June 2009, a unit waits in the platform before restarting its journey to Birmingham and beyond. *Barry Hilton/MJS*

Chapter 1
Kidderminster to Foley Park

Our railways are not just about engines and coaching stock, and preserved lines are no different. Signalling is one vitally important ingredient, not least to preserve the safety of both railway and travelling public. One element of this, especially where single-line working is involved, is the use of 'tokens', given to a driver to allow him to proceed onto such sections. This view inside Bewdley's signal box on 22 March 1958, when the line was still operated by British Railways, shows some of the machines in use and the 'tablets' that will be removed or fed into them at appropriate moments. *Gerald Adams, MJS collection*

Now on the platform inside the main line station, the access ramp on the eastern side is clearly seen, as a Derby-built WR three-car Suburban DMU set (later Class 116) – with DMS W50094 leading – enters with the 1.55pm Birmingham (Snow Hill)-Stourport service on Sunday 30 March 1958. Less than a year old at the time, the Driving Car was later renumbered 53094, before being sent to Mayer Newman's scrapyard in Snailwell, East Anglia, for incineration in May 1988. It is here adorned with the second BR-style logo on the bodyside and the attractive 'whiskers' that were the precursors of the fuller yellow ends that were to come.

Although obviously the same vantage point, there are various changes in this view from 12 June 2009. The ramp and bridge are extant, although both are being 'threatened' by the prodigious tree growth over the intervening 51 years; the running-in board has disappeared and passengers will now have to peer harder to see where they are; the canopy of this near-side platform has gone, replaced by a much smaller affair; and the length of this platform has been truncated in the station rebuilding. The water tower, seen just beyond the final coach above, has also gone. No 150014 enters the station with the 1002 London Midland service from Stourbridge Junction, which will terminate here. *Mike Mensing/MJS*

While it is not my normal policy to replicate pictures from previous volumes, I have here made an exception, as the 'present' view seen in the earlier volume has changed dramatically and the old route to Birmingham (Snow Hill) has also reopened. On Easter Saturday, 9 April 1977, the stock that will form the 1203 service to Lichfield enters from the sidings, comprising two three-car DMU sets – another '116' WR Suburban set in plain blue and a Met-Cam Class 101 set in grey with blue banding. The goods shed is in use by NCL and the adjacent yard is busy with, among other items, 16-ton open wagons and Railfreight box vans. Note the open nature of the new station, just a couple of years old.

The precise spot to replicate the earlier photograph has, sadly, been blocked by yet more tree growth, so this is slightly to the left. The two most obvious changes on 12 June 2009 are the very recent erection of the station footbridge and lifts, and the view to the horizon. Very few of the distant buildings seen in the 1977 shot are still standing, and the car park is now the preserve of the main-line clientele, with the SVR visitors using space on the far side of their line from this view. The relatively new SVR station can be seen encroaching into the view on the extreme right. No 150132, in predominantly blue livery, compared to the green garb of the unit on the previous page, enters the station with the London Midland 1006 service to Shirley, via Snow Hill. *Mike Mensing/MJS*

A couple of hundred yards south of the two stations now present in Kidderminster, a long footbridge forms the only crossing point of both railways. This gives superb vantage points for photography of either or both railways, looking north or south. In 1976 another grey/blue '116' unit makes its way towards the main-line station – just visible to the right of the goods shed – forming the 1650 Hereford-Birmingham (New Street) service, while a southbound unit stands in the platform and two three-car units wait in the sidings on the right. These sidings occupy the site of the first engine shed here, which closed in 1932.

Thirty years on and the developments to 12 June 2009 have been more subtle here than elsewhere. The unit types have changed, with the old first-generation types long gone; there has been housing expansion in the fields to the right; the water tower has had the old tank replaced with one of a much squatter profile; the sidings are no longer in use, with the line up to the end of the platform now removed; and the old corrugated-iron hut has gone from the side of the small hut on the left. The new station footbridge can be seen now in place and a second siding has been added to that on the left. *Mike Mensing/MJS*

Moving through some 45 degrees to the left, the view towards the former Comberton Hill goods yard, which is slowly being transformed for the new railway, looks rather spartan. All that remains from the site's BR heyday (see the next page) are the goods shed, water tank, coal storage bays and some of the buildings in the left distance. Elsewhere, things are changing, as track has been rationalised and realigned and a platform has been put into place by the fledgling SVR. The date is 1984 and No 37304 gingerly moves across from the main line to the preserved line with its precious cargo, No 3440 *City of Truro*.

The passage of time has served to soften the harshness of the earlier view, with bushes and trees growing on the preserved site; the squat water tank has replaced its predecessor; lighting has appeared in the yard; a signal box has been constructed by the restorationists; and the old goods shed has become the SVR's Carriage Repair Shop. In this undated view, probably from their visit in May 1991, Nos 20902 and 20903 top and tail a weedkilling train that is bringing its 'medicine' to the SVR. *Hugh Ballantyne/ David Johnson*

Top: The way we were! It is only from views like this, with the 'old' railway going about its daily business, that we realise just how much we have lost. Some would argue that, with the advent of the SVR, we have gained – and this is true in so many ways – but it cannot just be nostalgia that makes sights like this stir the blood. On 9 February 1965 No 6155 leaves the goods yard at Kidderminster with its impressively mixed rake of goods wagons, working hard as it lifts its load from the standing start. Note the coal merchants collecting their next loads, the railwayman (left of centre) grinning at the photographer, and the single coach dumped in the station sidings.

Above: On 12 June 2009 it is almost a picture of two halves! Right of centre, the main line is virtually unchanged; the goods shed and water tower still dominate, and the track to them, together with the turnout from the main line, is much as before, but beyond this to the left all is change, with the exception of the Railway Bell Hotel, in the centre distance. No 7812 *Erlestoke Manor* exits Kidderminster Town station – the SVR terminus – with the 1210 service for Bridgnorth. The realignment of the track in the erstwhile goods yard, since the arrival of the preserved railway, is obvious in this comparison, but such is the skill of the new railway in recreating a bygone age that it all looks as though it could always have been this way!
Colour-Rail.com/MJS

KIDDE

STER STATION SIGNAL BOX

Left: The previously seen new platform, installed by the developing SVR, is seen here at a closer angle, but again from the long footbridge. On 29 July 1984 ex-BR Class 08 shunter No D3022 helps with final preparations for the official opening on the following day. Still in BR green and externally looking very smart, it was a product of Derby Works in May 1953, as No 13022, later receiving a new identity as No 08015 in January 1974, under the BR TOPS numbering system. Withdrawal came from Tinsley (Sheffield) depot in September 1980 but, happily, it was to avoid the ignominious fate meted out to so many of its kin. Note the extensive temporary car park on the right and the 'landscaping' of the spoil from the platform construction.

Right: A case of déjà vu and serendipity! It is unusual for services to be interrupted by attention to the rolling stock, but while waiting for the next departure, to simulate the past view, I was rewarded by the very same '08' – D3022 – arriving to haul the 'Royal Scot' rake of coaches to the washing plant! This view from 12 June 2009, therefore, is a wonderful comparison of change over the last 25 years. The tracks to the left, Kidderminster Station Signal Box on the right, and the SVR's station building, complete with newly erected canopy, now partly obscuring the Railway Bell Hotel, are the most obvious additions. The right-hand car park is not solely for the main-line travellers; semaphore signals and watering facilities have been installed; and the proliferation of greenery serves to soften the overall view. *Hugh Ballantyne/MJS*

Left: By 7 October 1990 further progress has been achieved compared with the previous 'past' view. More landscaping has occurred, to allow tracks to progress towards the new platform, the signal box has been put in place and the station building appears at the far end. Visitor numbers have also grown, visible in this portrait of a famous locomotive. Drawing the onlookers in large numbers, ex-LNER 'A3' No 4472 *Flying Scotsman* heads the seven-coach 1440 departure to Bridgnorth, which is heaving with passengers, judging by the number of heads poking from carriage windows! Note the 'tongue-in-cheek' headboard, announcing the train as 'The Frying Scotsman'! *Hugh Ballantyne*

Above: By comparison, the much more diminutive ex-GWR No 1369 has just four coaches as it leaves with a lunchtime departure to Bewdley on Saturday 25 September 2005. The main other differences are the wheelsets stored alongside the running line and the completion of the trackwork into the station area. *Horace Gamble*

Top right: As has been seen, the SVR's 'Town' station developed considerably between the railway's official opening in 1984 and the arrival of *Flying Scotsman* in 1990. Although ersatz in creation and not replicating an original edifice, the design and outfitting were to result in a highly attractive arena. This view, at 1130 on 15 August 1987, shows the location newly laid out with seating and flower tubs, alongside the warm-coloured brick and the pseudo-GWR signage.

Centre: No business can stand still – progress is either forward or back. Like any successful enterprise, the SVR has not stopped thinking and planning ahead, and evidence of this can be seen from the same vantage point on 12 June 2009, 50 minutes and nearly 22 years on from the earlier view! The disabled room now also serves for baby-changing; a replica W. H. Smith kiosk has appeared; the window panes have received decoration; the seats have been moved; 'heritage' luggage and trolley adorn the concourse; and, most importantly in times of bad weather, an overall canopy, on substantial pillars, has appeared – complete with second clock and 'gas lamp' – finalised in 2008.

Below: Viewed from outside, from the still cobbled approach road, the design and 'antique' appearance are enhanced by mock-GWR poster boards and signage, and the windows and lamps mirror those inside. Built from scratch and opened in 1987, this certainly gives the approaching visitor a much stronger feeling of welcome than the nearby main-line structure. *Hugh Ballantyne/MJS (2)*

Above: Following the installation of the overall canopy, together with old-style gates at the end of the platform, the Town station now gives the impression to the arriving passenger of a seaside terminus, with all the anticipation that can come with that. This delightful mid-morning view on 11 August 2008 is completed with GWR seating, poster boards and 'shrubs in tubs'. *MJS*

Right: Here is another angle on the signal box and squat water tank provided by the SVR following its takeover of the site. On 17 April 1993 ex-BR No 42968 masquerades as LMS No 2968, complete with low-sided Fowler tender,

as it prepares to leave the Kidderminster environs and make the climb up the valley towards Bridgnorth. One of Stanier's derivatives of the LMS 'Crab' 2-6-0s, it emerged from Crewe Works in 1934, as LMS No 13268. Initially allocated to Willesden shed, it was swiftly moved north, to work from Edge Hill (Liverpool) shed in April 1935. After withdrawal from BR, by which time it had become 42968, it was sent to Barry for scrapping in March 1967. Happily it was preserved by the Stanier Mogul Fund, becoming the 45th escapee from Barry, in December 1973, with a later move to the SVR.

Opposite bottom: Moving a few yards away from the station platform, ex-GWR 2-6-2PT No 4566 arrives at Kidderminster on 12 June 2009 with a returning train from Bridgnorth. Ten years older than No 2968, appearing from Swindon Works in 1924, it was one of the later examples of the original '4500' Class, built to Churchward's design for branch-line work, with straight-topped tanks. Cornwall

was its home for all but six months of its BR life, with the end coming from Laira (Plymouth) shed on 21 April 1962. Having first been shipped to Barry for scrap, it was saved and moved to Bewdley in July 1970, where it was restored. Thus, in 2009, it has been in private hands longer than in service with BR. *Tom Heavyside/MJS*

Below: 11 August 2008 was an important day for UK railways, being 40 years from the end of steam on BR and the running of the infamous 1T57 'Fifteen Guinea Special'. To celebrate this milestone, one of the locomotives featured on that special was turned out by the SVR to haul a non-stop run from Kidderminster to Bridgnorth. In this portrait, moments before the departure, 'Black Five' No 45110 stands ready to enjoy the event. With his back to the engine, David Porter, who saved it from the scrapman all those years ago, talks of the salvation with Ron Lawson, winner of a *Steam Railway* competition for a cab ride. *MJS*

Below: A massive amount of freight was handled by BR during its lifetime, especially in the first two decades, and a comparable amount of land was occupied by sidings and marshalling yards to handle the various traffics. Views such as this were the norm in those heady days but are now much mourned by enthusiasts. Kidderminster's engine shed, situated in the distance beyond the sidings, was re-coded '2P' on 9 September 1963, when the area was taken over by the London Midland Region for its final 11 months to closure on 10 August 1964. No 4173, shunting coal wagons on 23 June 1964, less than two months from closure, has a painted version of the shedplate on the smokebox front, together with what looks to be a hand-made and painted front numberplate. One of Stourbridge's '08' diesel shunters – probably D3115, yard pilot on this date – pauses between duties on the left. The yard shunter waits with his pole, ready to couple up more wagons, and the whole operation and site is overlooked by the Kidderminster Junction signal box.

Right: Another picture of two halves! On the left the tracks and signal box are basically as of yore, with the exceptions of the absence of lines connecting the main and SVR lines and the reduction of the semaphore signal gantry to just one arm. To the right of the diesel shunter a new running line has been installed, together with a connection, and an impressive signal gantry controls traffic from the Bewdley direction and a turnout to the SVR's yard and relatively newly erected storage shed. On 12 June 2009 a nice link to the 'past' view below is D3022, which was a contemporary of the '08' standing by No 4173. *Colour-Rail.com/MJS*

Also seen from the long footbridge is 'Prairie' No 4153, a Kidderminster loco for all bar three months of its BR life. On 13 July 1964, a month from its final transfer to Stourbridge Junction shed, it is carefully snaking over the various points, bringing a long rake of empty coal wagons into the yard. The twin-track main line on the left heads for Stourport and Worcester, while the line to Bewdley, the erstwhile 'Kidderminster Loop', arcs right underneath the plume of smoke from another 'Prairie'. The whole is overlooked by the College of Further Education in the distance.

An interim view between 'past' and 'present' sees No 37304 again as it negotiates the junction, bringing *City of Truro* to the new railway. Much of the old trackwork is still extant but, with BR having ceased operations here in this year, reclamation of materials has begun.

Again the main and SVR running lines are much as before, but now lacking the previous connection. To the left, No 150010 is about to pass the 'Junction' signal box before moving onto the turnround siding beyond. To its right, No 7812 *Erlestoke Manor* – echoing No 4153 above by running tender-first – hauls its 'Royal Scot' rake of coaches past the shed yard with the 1010 departure from Bridgnorth. Note that the College has now disappeared and the scene is now dominated more by the Kidderminster Football Club's stadium.
Colour-Rail.com/Hugh Ballantyne/MJS

Although not absolutely essential, a turntable is a handy addition to a preserved steam centre. It primarily gives the ability to turn a locomotive to be facing forwards for a return journey, which can also be of great assistance in evening out the wear of tyres, etc. As seen in this view from 1992, in an unused corner, the preparatory work is under way to create such a facility within Kidderminster's shed yard. Two years later, George Law Ltd, of Kidderminster, installed a ring of concrete on which the turntable was to sit.

Originally new to Fort William in 1948, the turntable was obtained from BR in the 1970s by The Merchant Navy Preservation Society and transported to Horsted Keynes on the Bluebell Railway. It was never installed and a group of SVR volunteers completed its purchase in 1980, for £35,000, initially for Bewdley. After lengthy storage on the ex-Cleobury Mortimer branch, its was finally craned into position in its current place at Kidderminster on 12 April 1994. Seen from the ground on Saturday 25 September 2005, the ensuing 11 years have been well spent and the facility, complete with reserve tanks to assist with movement of the 70-foot table, has become part of the scenery. The view of No 9466 being turned in the early autumn sunshine makes for a very pleasing portrait. *Paul Chancellor, Colour-Rail.com/Horace Gamble*

Above: The railway climbs for a mile or so out of Kidderminster and, close to the summit, passes the site of Foley Park Halt. Opened in 1905, it was accessed by way of the A451 Kidderminster to Stourport road until its closure in 1970. In the foreground of this view, from 6 September 1969, some of the sidings associated with the nearby British Sugar Corporation site are rapidly being recolonised by nature. The section from the factory to Bewdley North ceased operation from 5 January 1970, although the stretch from Kidderminster lasted until April 1982. Being a Halt, passengers only were handled, with no facilities for parcels or any form of freight. Note the typical GWR-style 'pagoda' waiting shelter.

Below: Moments later a crowd has appeared to board the single-car diesel unit for the short run into Kidderminster. No evidence of this site now exists, or normal access to it. The exploration of a possible 'ultra-light' commuter service between Kidderminster and Bewdley, early in 2009, might have been enhanced if the Halt had still existed! Also during 2009, two of the large sugar beet silos were due to be dismantled brick by brick, as the threat to the railway was considered too great for the use of explosives! *Both Robin Leleux*

Chapter 2
Bewdley to Arley

After the summit, the line continues on a falling gradient of 1 in 100 and passes through Bewdley (or Foley Park) Tunnel and into open country. On 15 April 1978 No 7819 *Hinton Manor* mimics a GWR express train, with a typically curved headboard, announcing 'The Severn Valley Limited' service from Bridgnorth. Heads peer from the front coach on the approach to the tunnel mouth, and the fireman looks back to ensure there are no problems.

Above: **Close to the same spot, on Saturday 25 September 1993, we see another visitor with a headboard. This time, ex-LNER No 3442 *The Great Marquess* climbs the 1 in 100 gradient towards the Birchen Coppice escarpment and the tunnel, adorned with a 'West Highlander' headboard acknowledging the work that these locomotives did in the Scottish Highlands in BR days. Note the typical heathland flora at this part of the route.** *Tom Heavyside/Horace Gamble*

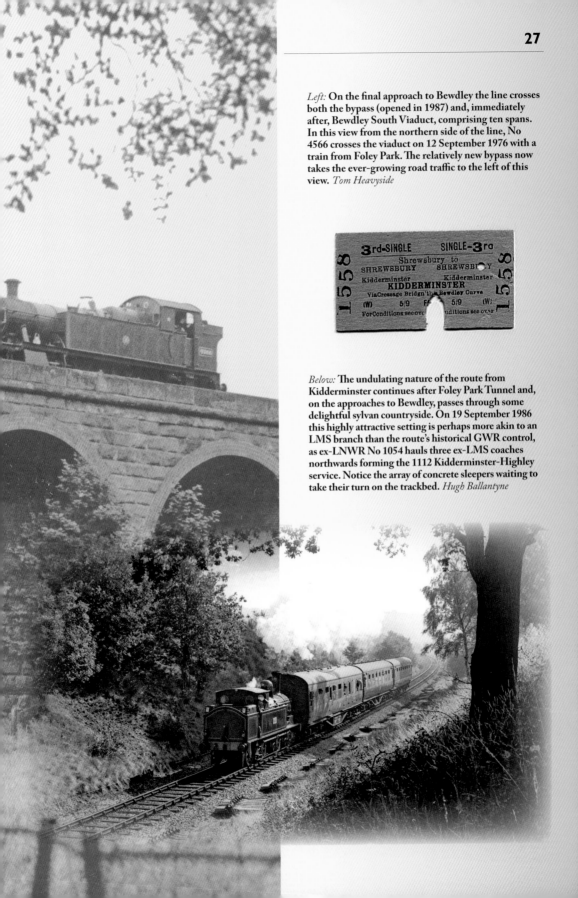

Left: On the final approach to Bewdley the line crosses both the bypass (opened in 1987) and, immediately after, Bewdley South Viaduct, comprising ten spans. In this view from the northern side of the line, No 4566 crosses the viaduct on 12 September 1976 with a train from Foley Park. The relatively new bypass now takes the ever-growing road traffic to the left of this view. *Tom Heavyside*

Below: The undulating nature of the route from Kidderminster continues after Foley Park Tunnel and, on the approaches to Bewdley, passes through some delightful sylvan countryside. On 19 September 1986 this highly attractive setting is perhaps more akin to an LMS branch than the route's historical GWR control, as ex-LNWR No 1054 hauls three ex-LMS coaches northwards forming the 1112 Kidderminster-Highley service. Notice the array of concrete sleepers waiting to take their turn on the trackbed. *Hugh Ballantyne*

Standing with his back to the viaduct seen on the previous page, the photographer captures ex-GWR 'Heavy Goods' No 2857 accelerating away from Bewdley station and about to obtain the single-line token from the signalman. The stately semaphore posts and signals guard the track from the south, protecting the 1320 Bridgnorth-Kidderminster service of 22 June 1986. New from Swindon Works in 1918, No 2857 arrived at Barry scrapyard in 1964, following withdrawal from Neath shed the previous year. It was to be 11 years before it was salvaged for the SVR, but has since given sterling service.

Twenty-three years later remarkably little has changed. Bewdley South signal box still controls all traffic, but there have been additions of Distant arms to the two posts, together with a diminutive 'calling-on' arm and a shallow smoke hood on the right-hand gantry. The 10mph speed restriction sign has disappeared and there has obviously been some weedkilling to control the grass on both sides of the line. On 13 June 2009 No 7802 *Bradley Manor* has been given a clear road, to run light-engine to Kidderminster, ready for the day's efforts. *Hugh Ballantyne/MJS*

Standing on the southern end of the island platform at Bewdley on 1 August 1960, ex-LMS 'Crab' No 42783 is an interloper onto the BR(W) metals, arriving with an excursion train from Rugeley, its nine-coach train snaking over the points on the approach. Some 3 miles from Kidderminster, Bewdley was an important railway location, being the terminus for two branches, from Stourport in the south (severed in 1973) and Tenbury Wells and Woofferton in the west (closed in 1962); the 'Prairie' tank on the left may well be en route to the former.

Here is another case of serendipity and good fortune, with No 7802 *Bradley Manor* arriving at Bewdley on 13 June 2009 with the 1105 Kidderminster-Bridgnorth working. Under normal circumstances 'up' trains pull into Platform 1, to the right of this view, but this service was diverted into Platform3, to accommodate a Luncheon train shortly due to arrive at the station, thus providing the ideal comparison to the earlier view. Bewdley was the southern terminus of the preserved line from 1974 to 1984, but has not lost its importance with the passage of time, as the site is the current railway's administrative headquarters and, with reasonable parking facilities, provides an alternative for joining the services. *David Johnson/MJS*

IN MEMORY OF
GARETH DAFYDD JONES
VOLUNTEER BOOKING OFFICE CLERK
AND TICKET INSPECTOR
SEVERN VALLEY RAILWAY

DIED SEPTEMBER 1983
AGE 28 YEARS

Left inset: **Turning through 180 degrees from the previous page, this is the view looking north at Bewdley on 18 August 1962. To the left a three-car DMU stands in Platform 2, waiting to work the 3.45pm local service to Birmingham (Snow Hill), while on the right No 3788 has just arrived from Shrewsbury. A little over a year later, on 2 December 1963, the route of No 3788's journey – the Severn Valley line between Alveley Sidings and the outskirts of Shrewsbury – closed to all traffic.**

Main picture: **Nearly five decades later the view on 13 June 2009 is incredibly similar. The 1105 Kidderminster-Bridgnorth service stands in Platform 3 on the right, going in the opposite direction from No 3788 above, and a chimney has disappeared from the station building on the left, but otherwise all is virtually the same, with some refreshed paintwork and strategic additions to the platform accentuating the attractiveness of the location. A signal has also been installed at the near end of Platform 1, to control access to the sidings. Flowerbeds and the generally tidy nature of the station all point to a railway and staff that care.** *Edwin Wilmshurst/MJS*

Although a former GWR route, the presence of ex-LMS locos was not unknown, especially in BR days. On Saturday 25 June 1960 Stanier Class 3 2-6-2T No 40126 slows for the stop at Bewdley with the 4.22pm Kidderminster-Shrewsbury stopper. With his engine having steam to spare, not being unduly taxed by the three-coach load, the fireman has time to check the passage into the platform. Note the mixed rake of DMU carriages about to travel in the opposite direction.

Seen from a little closer to the end of Platform 1, the trackwork is basically the same but the relatively peaceful ambience of 1960 is here replaced by one of activity. No 37 more modern and, indeed, more powerful motive power in of the first train of the day, the 0950 Kidderminster-Bridgn on Saturday 13 June 2009, while one of the old school, No *Bradley Manor* receives attention before the day's duties. *M Mensing/MJS*

Bewdley with a lightweight two-coach train, the 1.45pm to Kidderminster, which is also transporting an empty fish van, en route from Shrewsbury.

Below: With the view from the siding platform blocked by coaches, the third view is from the ground. On the dull early morning of 13 June 2009, the only material change is the installation of a semaphore signal at the southern end of Platform 1. Elsewhere, there is great credit to the present railway for the attention to detail in their preservation and the retention of character and style of the original station. *John Keylock/ Colour-Rail.com/MJS*

Top: **Turning through 180 degrees from the previous page, we are now looking towards Bridgnorth. In 1955 two of the later ex-GWR Railcar designs stand in Platforms 1 and 2 at Bewdley, on passenger duties between Shrewsbury and Hartlebury; the down train, on the left, has the white roof enhancement. Elsewhere, everything looks to be neat and tidy and well cared for, both on and off the tracks.**

Centre: **By 17 October 1962 nothing has changed, except for the removal of the wagon from the left-hand siding and the arrival of steam in place of diesel. No 41202 pauses at**

The attractive covered footbridge has been glimpsed in earlier images and we are now
on that bridge, looking down on the station towards Kidderminster on 21 August 1959.
Another ex-GWR Railcar stands in the platform awaiting the 'right away'. Presumably
any intending travellers are already aboard, as there are just two ladies remaining on the
platform and the porter is scurrying across the board crossing. This vista shows the full
extent of the sidings present at the station at this time. *Frank Hornby collection*

The GWR Railcars seen previously in 1955 are seen again, that on the right adorned
with white roof ends and early warning 'whiskers'. The one on the left could, conceivably, be
No W20W, which was still operating through Bewdley in 1958, but still without any front
warning markings.

Below: **By 6 September 1963 single-car diesels are still employed on the route, but they are now of more modern design. On the left, No W55005 waits to proceed with the 4.20pm Shrewsbury-Hartlebury service, while on the right No W55004 will travel north as the 6.24pm service to Bridgnorth from Hartlebury. Built by Gloucester C&W Ltd in May 1958, No 55004 was a Class 122 DMBS and survived, serving various outposts of the ex-GWR system, until withdrawal in October 1990. Its end came in the furnaces of Mayer Newman, Snailwell, the following month. In contrast, No W55005 worked until October 1992 and was then fortunate enough to be preserved. On the extreme left, a three-care unit waits to leave for Kidderminster in Platform 3, while it is loaded with parcels. The line closed officially the following Monday, the 9th.** *John Keylock/Hugh Ballantyne*

Above right: **All is tranquil in this comparative view captured very early in the morning on 31 July 2005. The sidings to the right of the main running lines are put to good use, being full of stored rolling stock in various stages of restoration. On the left can be seen one of the railway's 'whiskered' DMU sets, which looks to be in fine fettle and makes for an appropriate link with the past shots.** *Peter Townsend*

The view from the footbridge in the opposite direction, looking towards Bridgnorth, has long been a favourite for photographers. The elevated position, wide panorama, signal box and semaphores, and a variety of lines on which trains can be captured, all add to the end result. On 26 April 1958 BR Standard tank No 82008 illustrates the point as it enters Bewdley with its three-coach train operating as the 1.45pm Hampton Loade-Worcester service. The vintage seating, unusual signal gantry by the box and the period housing to the right all add their own charm.

Right: The combined talents of the SVR and Mother Nature have led to a wonderful recreation of past working. On 13 June 2009 the driver of No 4566 has slowed to surrender his single-line token, as his train of ex-LNER teak coaches approaches the station as the 1230 Bridgnorth-Kidderminster service. The practice of token exchange, together with the unusual signal gantry design, the trolleys and milk churns, all add to the evocation of the railway as it was, while the prodigious growth on either side of the line masks the surroundings and softens the overall feel of the location. *R. J. Buckley, Initial Photographics/Shu-Ju Lee*

Left: **Down at platform level, 'Mickey Mouse' No 41202, already seen in an earlier picture, is now glimpsed moments before, with the fireman about to surrender his token to the signalman as the 1.45pm departure from Shrewsbury arrives at Bewdley on 17 October 1962. New from Crewe Works in December 1946, for the LMS as No 1202 and the third of the Ivatt design, it was renumbered 41202 by the new British Railways in November 1948. Initially allocated to Abergavenny shed, it stayed there until a move to Bristol (Bath Road) in March 1955. Allocated to Shrewsbury when seen here, it was a well-travelled engine, eventually ending up at Stockport (Edgeley), from where it was withdrawn on 3 December 1966 – exactly 20 years old. Note the '6 Car' notice under the left-hand signal, for the benefit of drivers of that length of DMU, and the evidence of the onset of autumn, with fires warming many houses to the right.** *Colour-Rail.com*

Right: In the latter years of through services over the route, 'Standard 3' 2-6-2Ts were drafted in to handle traffic. On 29 April 1961 No 82005 waits to leave Bewdley with the 4.35pm train to Shrewsbury. Just short of ten years old when seen here, it had been sent new to Tyseley but spent a truly nomadic existence, sometimes moving more than once within a year. Newly transferred to Shrewsbury when operating this train, it has not yet received the relevant '89A' shedplate in this view. The final move was to the Southern Region and a very short stay, of just 4 ½ months, at Nine Elms shed. It finally returned to Wales, to be cut at Birds Commercial Motors Ltd, Risca, in February 1966.

Below: Again we view a 'Mickey Mouse' in the station. On 13 June 2009 No 46443

slows at Bewdley for its driver to receive the single-line token for his Dining Special from Kidderminster to Bridgnorth. The platform has been graced with attractive tubs; the footbridge has been repainted and re-roofed; the staff stand ready for any eventualities; and, again, the whole is a very pleasing scene. *David Johnson/Tom Heavyside/MJS*

Opposite botom: For ten years, from 1974 to 1984, Bewdley was the southern terminus of the new SVR. During that period, on 4 April 1982, No D1013 *Western Ranger* eases from the station, the focus of much attention, with the 1230 train to Bridgnorth. The seating arrangements, running-in sign and other notices are all different from BR days – and the left-hand gantry has lost an arm – but the station still retains much of its original charm.

Immediately on leaving the station for the north, trains negotiate Bewdley North (or Wribbenhall) Viaduct. Comprising eight arches, it towers over the A456 Kidderminster-Ludlow road and the surrounding dwellings. On 18 August 1974 Bewdley was the new terminus from Bridgnorth and No 43106 is seen running round its train before returning north. New on 24 March 1951, weighing 99 tons and the last of the class to be built at Darlington Works, it was an Eastern Region engine until moving to Saltley shed in March 1962. Remaining on the London Midland Region thereafter, it was to succumb to the inevitable on 13 July 1968, from Lostock Hall, just three weeks from the end of steam on BR. Happily, preservation beckoned and, now affectionately known as 'The Flying Pig', a return from a long overhaul on the SVR in 2009, more than 20 years since it last saw active service! *Tom Heavyside*

After crossing the viaduct, the route appeared in BR days to be double track, but was in fact two single lines. The left-hand line became the Wyre Forest line to Tenbury Wells and Woofferton Junction, crossing the River Severn on Dowles Bridge as it swung away at Northwood towards its destination; the piers of this bridge were still intact in 2009. This route closed on 30 July 1962 but is seen neat and tidy and ready for service in this view from 20 June 1959. Another 'Standard 3', No 82004 is seen operating as the three-coach 1.45pm Shrewsbury-Hartlebury local service on the undulating Severn Valley route, here on the shallow embankment segregating it from its neighbour.

That embankment is still intact, and the much steeper escarpment to the right, with its trees, is as before, but the rails have long since disappeared from the Tenbury line. On 13 June 2009 'Growler' fans enjoy their journey behind No 37906 as it heads for Bewdley as the 1145 Bridgnorth-Kidderminster service. *Michael Mensing/ MJS*

Looking back towards Bewdley, the falling gradient of the Wyre Forest line is readily apparent. With the Distant signals set against both roads, No 3769 makes its way cautiously with the 1.45pm Shrewsbury-Hartlebury service on Saturday 15 August 1959, composed of a mixed rake of Western Region coaches. A local engine for the whole of its BR existence, being, respectively, at Tyseley, Wolverhampton (Stafford Road), Wrexham and Shrewsbury, it was at the latter shed when seen here, and stayed there until withdrawal in October 1962.

Leaning into the task ahead, No 7812 *Erlestoke Manor* travels in the opposite direction at the head of the 1235 Kidderminster-Bridgnorth turn on 13 June 2009. The hot summer sun creates deep shadows and swallows the engine's exhaust. At 16 miles, the SVR is the second-longest of the ex-Western lines, after the West Somerset Railway, and thus the erstwhile express locomotives have a chance to stretch their legs and show themselves to advantage. *Michael Mensing/MJS*

This view of our previous location is from the other side of the River Severn on 15 April 1978, as No 47383 makes its way from Bewdley en route for Bridgnorth. The foreground shows the four pillars of the old Dowles Bridge still standing, with the attractive honey-coloured bricks highlighting their design. The 'Manor' snapped on the previous page is at approximately the point of the last carriage of the five behind No 47383. While the piers still stand in and around the water, this view is now unobtainable due to the prolific accretion of surrounding trees and foliage. *Ben Ashworth*

Roughly a mile north of the old junction, Northwood Halt was a small wayside station, with a single short platform to serve only passengers, without any facilities for goods traffic. Reached along the single-track Northwood Lane from that junction, it was perched on a narrow ledge on a steep hillside, as can be seen, surrounded by trees and with precious little habitation nearby. On 29 April 1961 No 82005 is bunker first as it arrives with the 3.36pm Shrewsbury-Hartlebury train, with what seems to be a healthy number of travellers waiting, considering the isolation of the site.

Discovering the location of the Halt is not easy for the uninitiated or unwary, and, situated immediately to the north of a narrow level crossing over a side road from Northwood Lane, parking is distinctly restricted in the 21st century! On 13 June 2009 No 4566 replicates the bunker-first earlier view as it glides slowly past what is now a 'request stop', with the driver of the 1230 Bridgnorth-Kidderminster service looking somewhat suspiciously at your photographer! Gone are the two rudimentary waiting shelters of earlier times, replaced by a recreation of a typical GWR corrugated-iron 'pagoda' edifice, and the situation is an ideal place to enjoy tranquillity, have a spot of lunch and watch the passing trains! Note the rake of ex-LNER teak coaches behind the 'Prairie'. *David Johnson/MJS*

Left: Arley station is another isolated location, but also one of the most picturesque on the line, situated on a hill on the west side of the Severn. The village (actually Upper Arley) is on the other side of the river, requiring a ferry journey to catch a train! Opened with the line in January 1862, it was initially a single line and platform, but traffic dictated that a loop, signal box and second platform be installed in 1883. Further alterations came in 1907, when the platforms were lengthened, and this view is around a year later, with the extensions seen at the far end. The signal box contained 14 levers.

Below: There are many locations along the SVR that provide attractive and/or impressive views, and Victoria Bridge is one such. Situated almost halfway between Northwood Halt and Arley, the foundation stone was laid on 24 November 1859. Named 'Victoria Bridge' in honour of the Queen, it was cast and erected by the Coalbrookdale Company and had the world's largest clear cast-iron span at the time. After the reopening of the line in 1969, it was extensively repaired by the SVR ten years later, with the work being completed in time for the new season, on 1 March 1980. Although away from public highways, it is easily accessed by walkers, but they would be well advised to choose a fine day, as it involves a long walk alongside the river! On 28 September 1985 No 2857 handles the 1432 Highley-Bewdley turn, the second of three freight trains run during an Enthusiasts' Weekend. *Hugh Ballantyne*

Above: The presence of Victorian gentlemen on the platform might indicate another view from that period, but this is misleading! Like so many other preserved railways, the SVR has entertained film crews, drawn to recreate past scenes, and here the date is 10 May 1983, with crew and actors caught during the production of *The Fasting Girl*, a dramatisation by Paul Ferris of newspaper reports of a young girl in South Wales in 1869 who was claimed to have fasted, without appreciable loss of health, for more than a year. Arley was renamed 'Pencader' for the production. Special rolling stock was brought in and No 7812 *Erlestoke Manor* was used as motive power. No 92220 *Evening Star* can just be seen beyond the station building, marooned for the week by the filming! *MJS collection/Hugh Ballantyne*

Below: A view from nearly 50 years later shows just how much the SVR has achieved in its preservation and development of the site. As No 4566 arrives on 13 June 2009, with the 1405 Kidderminster-Bridgnorth train, the ambience is from a different world. Admittedly aided by warm summer sunshine, the feel of the station is now attractive, welcoming and pleasurable. Families are catered for, with picnic tables and a shop, and the platform 'gardens', clean paintwork, plenty of seating and the overhanging trees all add their parts to the visitor's jigsaw. *MJS collection/MJS*

Above: When the route opened in 1862, all the stations (except Bridgnorth) were constructed to a basic design, providing booking office-cum-waiting room, toilet facilities, Station Master's accommodation and a minimum of one siding. This was lavish for many, where the passenger throughput was probably only sufficient for wayside halt status. One such was Arley, and the basic building design can be seen on the up platform as No 4629 arrives with its three-coach 'local'. The view is undated but would have been between January 1961, when Kidderminster shed was redesignated as '84G' (note the shedplate bearing this code on the locomotive), and January 1963, when No 4629 was transferred away to Gloucester. In any case, it was relatively close to the closure of the through route, which came in September 1963, and the lack of intending passengers on the platform as the train arrives bears out the low demand here.

Left: 'Mickey Mouse' No 46443 (seen earlier at Bewdley) is again the focus, but this time masquerading as LMS No 6443, in unlined black livery. With steam to spare, it awaits the 'right away' at Arley on 28 August 1979, temporarily delayed by the young lad holding open the carriage door! The entrance to the sidings can be seen on the left, together with fencing protecting the public, and the signal box beyond.

Right: A comparative view from closer to the line shows the need for the locomotive to be beyond the platform end, to allow the longer length of train to fit into the platform. On 13 June 2009 No 4566 is again seen with its 1405 departure from Kidderminster, enhanced by its delightful rake of superbly clean teak coaches. The entrance to the sidings is still to the left, with a signal in place to control movements. *Bryan Hicks/MJS*

Chapter 3
Highley to Hay Bridge

Highley is another out-of-the-way station, but not so isolated from its eponymous community as Arley. Some 9 ½ miles from Kidderminster, it was originally equipped with just one platform, and this is how it has stayed, unlike others on the route. There were once four collieries in close proximity, all rail-connected. Kinlet and Billingsley, whose sidings were a mile or so south of the station, closed in 1935 and 1922 respectively; Highley, whose siding left the station immediately to the south, effectively ceased production in 1940; and Alveley, which opened in 1940, some quarter of a mile north of the station, took over. Both the latter were officially closed early in 1969. This view from 17 April 1959, looking south from the station footbridge, shows the colliery branch diverging to the right, with wagons in the middle distance.

With the original footbridge having succumbed to age and demolition in 1974, the comparative view is from the ground. On 20 June 2009 the approach road to the station is still in situ, as is the cattle dock, now 'rebuilt', the signals and the brick hut on the right. The former colliery branch is also in place, but now leads to the newly opened Engine House museum. Note the installation of a water tank. *H. C. Casserley/MJS*

Left: This view shows early preparatory work on the site for The Engine House museum on 28 August 2006. Part financed by the European Union, with money from the European Regional Development Fund, support was also received from Bridgnorth District Council, Advantage West Midlands and the Heritage Lottery Fund, and it is reassuring to note that these organisations saw the potential benefits of the project. Climbing the path above the old mining siding, the view back towards the main running line clearly outlines the building's early footprint. The size of the task, including clearing unwanted undergrowth and landscaping, can be judged from this angle.

Right: On the dull morning of 20 June 2009 it can be seen that construction is over and the museum is ready for business. Note the twin tracks entering the facility, roughly along the alignment of the old sidings, and strategic parking for the disabled visitor. *Paul Chancellor/MJS*

Left: The final approach to Highley station from the Kidderminster direction shows the layout virtually unchanged over its long history. The station building and its attendant single platform have survived progressive developments and, as seen on 20 June 2009, is now under care from the SVR. The ex-colliery loop lines are still in place, as is the site's signalbox. 25 years after the demolition of the original footbridge, the skeleton of a replacement are firmly in place.

Right: Just four months later and the istallation of the bridge is complete - aided by £25,000 of grants - though not yet opened to the public.   Not only will the new facility provide a safer crossing of the lines by the public, but also it will enable photographers to have a fresh vantage point. This view is from 17 October 2009. *Both MJS.*

In another view from the embankment over the colliery sidings, this time we are looking north towards Bridgnorth. On 15 April 1978 No 7819 *Hinton Manor* eases forward, restarting its 'Severn Valley Limited' Bridgnorth-Bewdley train. This vantage point graphically demonstrates the curving nature of the site, the single platform and the two lengthy sidings. It is also without a footbridge, visitors reverting to the original practice of accessing the platform by a wooden barrow crossing. The unusually full sidings show both the limited space available for storage on the railway at this time and the amount of stock already in hand, ready for restoration over time.

With the previous vantage point now unavailable, this view is from the balcony of the Engine House museum on 7 March 2010. The new footbridge is in the background as Nos 4566 and 5764 restart their journey south during the railway's 'Spring Steam Reunion Gala'. *Ben Ashworth/MJS*

Above: Another view of a train leaving Highley for Bewdley, on 11 September 1976, sees No 4566 accelerate with a rake of coaches filled with eager enthusiasts, judging by the number of heads at the windows! At that time 52 years old, being new from Swindon Works in 1924, the straight-topped tanks of the original design, already commented upon, are clearly seen from this angle. The railway's mobile crane stands to the right of the signal box.

Right: The comparative view on 20 June 2009 shows no change to the track or the two signals on either side, but otherwise a water tank has appeared and the cattle dock has been renovated and rejuvenated, but the telegraph pole adjacent to the right-hand signal has gone. The proliferation of ferns on the nearside embankment has also been cleared. *Tom Heavyside/MJS*

Opposite page top: This may be 11 September 1976, but the provision of a vintage steam locomotive in period costume, telegraph pole and gas lamp give the sense of a GWR branch line. No 5764 is about to pass the barrow crossing as it approaches Highley station with a Bewdley-Bridgnorth train. Originally from Swindon Works in 1929,

it was sold to London Transport in May 1960, following withdrawal from Old Oak Common shed. Renumbered L95, it moved to LT's depot at Neasden, from where it worked across London. That might have been the end, but happily, having been discarded by LT, it was saved and brought to the SVR in 1971.

Right: Time moves on, even for heritage railways, and diesels have become both useful alternatives to steam, sometimes at lower cost, and a draw for the younger enthusiasts who never knew steam in its pre-1968 days. The need to carry a token on a single lines, however, is still as relevant

today as previously, and the practice of exchanging between loco crew and signalman is here exemplified, as Class 50 No D444 *Exeter* slows for the handover on 20 June 2009, while operating the 0950 Kidderminster-Bridgnorth service, the first train of the day. *Tom Heavyside/MJS*

Seen from the footbridge on 17 April 1959, the station building at Highley is imposing, partly due to the fact that it was built using stone, probably from a local quarry, rather than brick as used elsewhere on this branch. While to the same basic design – a substantial quasi-Victorian home with smaller working and waiting facilities – there were subtle differences along the route and, compared to its neighbour at Hampton Loade, this view shows a longer body to the main building and to the lower 'extension'. Note the presence of two prams, one obviously with a passenger and the other presumably the property of the Station Master.

Again viewed from the ground, in the absence of a footbridge, the station buildings are little changed but now look smarter and more 'cared for', with attractive flowerbeds by the main structure, a new lamp to light the platform, some replacement of slates on the roof and bricks on the underside of the platform, improved seating on the platform, and a display of milk churns at the far end. Two volunteers arrive at the station on 20 June 2009, to open up and make ready for the day. *Richard Casserley/MJS*

Right: **Nostalgia is a powerful emotion and one that has increased in value and intensity into the 21st century, where 'heritage' has become both a buzzword and a magnet. It is human nature to look back at so-called golden days, and on preserved railways the era of steam is an example. On 21 June 1986 the SVR at Highley has pulled out all the stops, with the period station complete with metal advertising signs and a vintage ex-LMS 'Jinty' on view. It stands in the middle road, waiting for a path into the platform, before taking a train to Bewdley. In unlined black and with a '26A' (Newton Heath) shedplate, it is redolent of the period when it was actually shedded there in 1966, but ... for the purists, the shed code at that time was '9D' and the tank-side BR logo should have been the later 'ferret and dartboard' rather then the 'cycling lion' seen here!** *Tom Heavyside*

Opposite top: **Moving through the station, to the northern end, the view looks rather sombre on a dull and misty 17 April 1959. Wagons for the colliery stand on the right, while the station patiently awaits the next train arrival and influx of travellers. The station access road can be seen sweeping down in the distance.**

Below: A clearer day and uncluttered track undoubtedly help, but on 20 June 2009 the view and ambience are eminently more appealing than in the earlier scene. The signal box is tastefully painted in the railway's colours and the station is far more picturesque and attractive, with garden, neatly painted sign and lamp posts, 'heritage' notice board and advertisement for Fry's Chocolate. The access road is still in situ but partially hidden here by the newly restored cattle dock fencing. *Richard Casserley/MJS*

As mentioned previously, Railcar No W20W was a regular on the Severn Valley route and is seen here at Highley on Saturday 25 June 1960, entering the station with the 7.55pm Bridgnorth-Stourbridge Junction working. When inherited by British Railways in 1948, it was working in and around Weymouth. With the limited seating capacity, there was obviously no anticipation of a huge demand for this service! Note that the rather decorative poster on the right is trying to escape!

When poised to take the comparative portrait on 20 June 2009, the cloud was widespread, but your photographer was blessed by a sudden burst of sunshine just as the train approached! No 7714 makes a wonderful recreation of a GWR branch-line train as it sweeps round the approach curve to the station with the 1100 Bridgnorth-Kidderminster service, consisting of 'Royal Scot' LMS coaches. New in 1930, from Kerr Stuart & Co Ltd in Stoke-on-Trent, the locomotive spent the whole of its BR life at Birkenhead, from where it was withdrawn on 27 December 1958. Then sold on to the NCB, it worked latterly at Penallta Colliery, Ystrad Mynach, in South Wales, before being dispensed with in December 1971. Initially preserved on the South Devon Railway, it has been an SVR servant for many years. *Michael Mensing/MJS*

Two miles north of Highley, Hampton Loade is another station off the beaten track, with its village again across the Severn, by ferry! Initially with a single platform, it was provided with two from 1882, thus becoming a strategic passing place on the route. It was the first to be extensively renovated by the fledgling railway, between 1967 and 1970, and was the southern terminus from the latter year until the extension was opened to Bewdley in 1974. Making use of this loop, two SVR trains pass on 22 August 1976. No 46521 slows for its stop while, on the right, the tanks of No 4141 lie awaiting restoration.

Three decades later D444 *Exeter*, seen from the platform, provides more up-to-date motive power, arriving on 20 June 2009 with the 1145 Bridgnorth-Kidderminster train. Seating and lamp standards have been replaced; a coach has been inserted at the end of the siding, between box van and vintage carriage – which bears the legend 'Carriage & Wagon Dept Taunton' on the board over the side door – and the previous open space to the right has been turned over to restoration of another vintage coach. D444 slows for the stop but, sadly, the brakes could not then be released, leading to around an hour's delay before 'Thunderbird' D8188 arrived from Kidderminster, summoned as rescue for the stricken train. Not surprisingly, the timetable was severely disrupted for the rest of the day. *Frank Hornby/MJS*

Opposite top: Built in 1862, Hampton Loade station remained unaltered though to closure in 1963, without the extension of the waiting room or other detail differences seen at Highley. On 17 April 1959, only the addition of the corrugated hut was 'new'! The station looks peaceful but, also, rather unkempt, illustrating the latter years of its existence and a possible lack of interest from BR. Its close proximity to the river and the ferry, however, made it a popular place to visit.

Left: The ill-fated D444, just seen, is here captured a few moments before the previous photograph, arriving with everyone blissfully unaware of what was about to happen! The basic structures and layout of the station on 20 June 2009 are the same as in BR days, with the exception of the redesign of the roof of the 'Gents', posters on the corrugated hut, new

lamp standards, the replacement of two chimney pots, a massive amount of tree growth, platform 'gardens' and the benefit of updated painting and signs. *Richard Casserley/MJS*

Above: The failure of D444 mentioned on the previous page provided a, thankfully, rare site of a rescue. In a sort of 'art imitating life', the railway's 'Thunderbird' loco on this day, D8188, finally restarts the stricken train from Hampton Loade, dragging D444 behind it; the service is now an hour behind schedule. The juggling of the remaining services and the limited number of crossing places for up and down trains was challenging for the various elements of control, but time was gradually recovered as the day wore on. D8188 took over D444's roster, in turn giving enthusiasts unexpected opportunities to travel behind it. *MJS*

Above: As noted earlier, Hampton Loade was the southern terminus for the first four years of the emergent SVR, until 1974, and this view portrays this status on 12 September 1971. 'Mickey Mouse' No 46443, here in BR lined black livery complete with 'ferret and dartboard' emblem on the tender, has run round its train and begins its return journey to Bridgnorth. Note the basic single-line arrangement with passing loop, and the signal bracket currently devoid of arms.

Below: Forward nearly 40 years and the situation looks very different on 20 June 2009. Together with the previously seen

proliferation of greenery, the signals are now fully part of the scene, as are the station staff waiting to transfer the single-line token from No 4566, arriving with the late-running 1230 Bridgnorth-Kidderminster train, the delay from the failure of D444 now reduced to 49 minutes due to smart work by the operating section. The scene is appreciated by young and old and by both sexes, and is completed by GWR-style signage. *Bryan Hicks/MJS*

Below left: Standing between the tracks at the northern end of the station, this was the view towards Highley on 17 April 1959, reinforcing the prosaic and misty conditions.

Below: Moments after the 'present' view on the previous page, No 4566 has successfully brought its train into the up platform on 20 June 2009, tailed by the 'observation car', while on the right No 7802 *Bradley Manor* waits to restart its turn as the 'SVR Footplate Experience' driver training special. The improvements wrought by the SVR – and nature – over the years are self-evident, especially the softening of the previously sparse appearance by the arboreal magnitude on either side of the line, the smartening of the station and the presence of dutifully attired staff. Note also that the Waiting Room on the left has been extended towards the platform edge, to make its profile flush with the rest of the building. *Richard Casserley/MJS*

In the very early days of the line reaching Hampton Loade, some parking was available on the approach to the old Station Master's house, as can be seen on 25 May 1970 as No 3205 returns towards its train (to the right of this view) before leaving for the relatively short run to Bridgnorth. In those relatively carefree days, both the parking and the cars' inhabitants are relaxed, a young lad being held aloft to witness the event – one wonders where he is now and whether he may have returned to the SVR as a volunteer!

By 17 August 1974 things are far more ordered. The driveway has now been gated, with parking provided on the opposite, Severn, side of the line. The old station approach road is now a private access. 'Flying Pig' No 43106 approaches with its service from Bridgnorth, past the relatively newly installed signals. *Ben Ashworth/Tom Heavyside*

SEVERN VALLEY RAILWAY

*Special ticket issued to mark five years
of the Severn Valley Railway as a volun-
tary organisation and the REOPENING
OF THE RAILWAY 23rd MAY 1970*

BRIDGNORTH
EARDINGTON
HAMPTON LOADE
AND RETURN

FIRST CLASS   **FARE 9/-**

0001

2nd-   CHEAP
             DAY

BRIDGNORTH
TO
SHREWSBURY
via Cressage

(W)
For Conditions see over

4233

Right: A move away from the station to a vaunted perch reveals the lie of the land at the station in the heady days of the reopening to this location. No 43106 is again seen, but this time on 25 May 1970, approaching its train, which can be glimpsed in the platform. A knot of passengers/onlookers gathers on the other platform, while others seemingly wander anywhere! The alternative parking at this date can be seen on the far side of the line and this view shows the proximity of the Severn beyond, apparently at low tide! As with other parts of the line, this vantage point is no longer available for viewing the railway, due to the growth of the trees. *Ben Ashworth*

Below: With the opening to Bewdley in 1974, the resident and visiting locomotives could begin to really stretch their legs and visitor numbers continued to increase, due to the longer ride and the greater variety in services. On 16 April 1977 we see No 46443 again, leaving Hampton Loade with a Bewdley-Bridgnorth train; there is a GWR anti-trespass notice to the left and a shorter, cautionary, SVR one to the right of the line. The main parking is now totally on the river side of the station.

Above: The passage of time has brought about much change, not least in the spread and depth of the brambles in the bottom right-hand corner of the earlier view, leading to this comparative shot being slightly lower down and closer to the station! No 7802 *Bradley Manor*, already seen with the 'Driving Experience' train, now leaves the station on its run north on 20 June 2009. To the left, the signal gantry, 10 mph sign, milepost and GWR trespass sign (with a 1932 Right of Way Act notice now above it) are still as before; the telegraph pole on the extreme left is now draped in ivy, while the one to the left of the loco has five cross beams rather than three; a new building has appeared, immediately to the left of No 7802; and a new TV aerial has been affixed to the chimney of the house on the right. Elsewhere, yet more tree growth has restricted the views and removed the very open feel of yesteryear. *Tom Heavyside/MJS*

Travelling north from Hampton Loade, the line threads a north-west curve between the River Severn on its right and Chelmarsh Reservoir to the left. Roughly three-quarters of the way along it passes over the B4555 Highley-Bridgnorth road at Hay Bridge. This was a favourite vantage point for many photographs in the first two decades of the new line and did provide a change of view, as can be seen in the portrait of No 3442 *The Great Marquess* about to cross the bridge on Saturday 22 April 1989, with another Kidderminster-Bridgnorth train. Compared with earlier views, the railway has not only removed much undergrowth on both sides of the line, but also some old fencing and a telegraph pole (to the right of the third coach).

Inset: Moving to the other side of the bridge and swinging through 180 degrees, No 3205 is seen in plain green livery on the bridge in the very earliest days, 15 April 1968. Built in 1946, the ex-GWR 0-6-0 was a much-travelled loco, initially to sheds on a Gloucester-Worcester-Shrewsbury-Machynlleth axis before decamping to Hereford in January 1963. Withdrawal came a month later, followed by reinstatement and a move to Exmouth Junction in December of that year. Staying in Devon, it finally succumbed on 13 August 1965, at Templecombe, but was saved for preservation on the South Devon Railway. It has subsequently continued its nomadic existence. *Horace Gamble/Bryan Hicks*

Chapter 4
Eardington to Bridgnorth

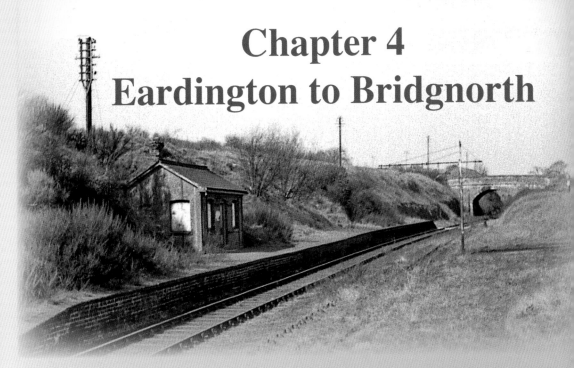

The climb to Eardington, a couple of miles from Hampton Loade, at 1 in 100, was sometimes a struggle for the less powerful motive power often used on the line, and restarting from the station en route for Bridgnorth would have tested both steed and driver. When seen on 27 March 1966, the facility had been closed for 2 ½ years and Nature is gaining ground in reclaiming the site. While isolated from any sizeable community, it was a very busy station at its height, catering for workers at the nearby Upper and Lower Forges, situated on either side of the line, and right up to closure a siding accompanied the single platform.

Not all progress is backward, and this illustration from 20 June 2009 shows what advances and improvements have been brought by the SVR. Though still closed, with much of its erstwhile platform removed and 'landscaped', the railway has retained a short length and has also installed a water tower and reinstated the siding. On this day the siding holds a very full ballast wagon, as well as other items. Note that the station building has been restored to something like its original state, though now missing the enamel advertisements that once graced the structure.
D. Bott/MJS

Above: Standing at the other end of the station and looking back towards Bewdley on 17 April 1959, the location appears in much better shape, four years from the end. The bogie bolsters chained with steel in the siding, the loading gauge beyond and the station building and station sign wearing a cared-for look, all point to work in progress.

Below: On 20 June 2009 the station building, now repainted, the slightly unusual telegraph pole behind it, the station sign echoing its predecessor and the reappearance of the siding all speak of 'TLC', but the rampant fern forest, hiding the wire fencing, and the trees sprouting on the far embankment betray the passage of time! Sadly, the loading gauge has disappeared. *H. C. Casserley/MJS*

Left: The B4555 executes almost a 90-degree left-hand bend from the alignment seen on the left in order to cross over the railway on its way to Bridgnorth. The view from that road bridge on 2 December 1979 sees No 5764 truly at home on this ex-GWR branch, but there is to be no stopping here on this date. A 'Santa Special' from Hampton Loade to Bridgnorth steams straight through Eardington, nearing the summit of the climb from Hampton Loade, after which it will coast down a 1 in 100 gradient to its destination.

Below: We have already seen the rescue of failed No D444 by 'Thunderbird' D8188. The unexpected appearance of the latter locomotive on this day, taking over the other diesel's roster, is not lost on the enthusiasts in the front coach, with their heads and cameras out to savour and capture the moment. On 20 June 2009 the Class 20 purrs through the station with the 1320 Kidderminster-Bridgnorth service, now with the late deficit down to 35 minutes. *Frank Hornby/MJS*

Our final look at Eardington is from the platform. On 17 April 1959 the station is still open as No 82004 slows for the stop with the 1.45pm Shrewsbury-Kidderminster working. New, to Tyseley, on 17 May 1952, the 'Standard 3' 2-6-2T moved to Barry in October 1953, then Newton Abbot in April 1955, before returning to the West Midlands in August 1956. Three years later – six months after this view – it transferred to Bath (Green Park) shed, from where it was dispensed with on 7 November 1965, just 13 ½ years old. No preservation beckoned for this loco, however, being cut at R. & S. Hayes (later Birds Commercial Motors), Bridgend, in February 1966.

Fifteen years later, on 17 August 1974, the SVR has tidied the station, reinstated the siding and has a pile of blocks, on the right, ready for more work. No 46521 looks very smart as it passes through with the 1545 Bridgnorth-Hampton Loade train. Interestingly, as an unintended link to the above view, the '88C' shedplate on the 'Mickey Mouse' is that of Barry! *H. C. Casserley/Tom Heavyside*

A quarter of a mile north of Eardington, No 82001 negotiates the 1 in 100 gradient of Eardington Bank on 30 August 1962, with the 1.45pm Shrewsbury-Kidderminster local service. Note how the railway has been carved through the escarpment. The second member of the Class, 'No 1' was new on 30 April 1952, going first to Tyseley shed. A long catalogue of meanderings around the southern and western quarters of the UK then followed, beginning on 3 October 1953 with a move to Barry. Thereafter, Devon, Bristol, Chester, Templecombe, South Wales, Exmouth Junction and Taunton all gave refuge before the end came at Bristol (Barrow Road) on 15 January 1966. The oxy-acetylene was quickly wielded thereafter, at Cashmore's scrapyard in Newport, South Wales, two months later.

Echoing the earlier view, with the loco facing north, No 46443 is a few yards further along on 18 July 1971, climbing with the 1400 Bridgnorth-Hampton Loade turn, comprising double the length handled by No 82001. The ensuing nine years have seen some marginal growth on the lineside, but this would accelerate over the subsequent three decades. *Michael Mensing/Edwin Wilmshurst*

Left: A prize for anyone who can accurately guess the date? North of Eardington Bank, the railway was carved through the hillside and sits within a deep cutting. The height and steep nature of this can be seen as No 5164 emerges from Knowlesands Tunnel, which runs under the B4555 road, with a 1315 Bridgnorth-Bewdley train. The loco is in pre-BR condition, but sans the buffer beam number, and wears the GWR 'shirt button' emblem on the tank … and the coaches could be chocolate and cream. But far from being in GWR days, the recreation of the past is superbly achieved by the SVR on 13 April 1980! *Hugh Ballantyne*

Below: Approaching Bridgnorth, the next major structure is Oldbury Viaduct, a five-span structure regnant in yet more undulating

countryside. With the town just visible in the upper right corner, No 3205 gains speed on the rising gradient on 15 April 1968. Note the double width of the viaduct, a legacy of the original plan by an abortive Wolverhampton-Bridgnorth scheme. Once again, with the tremendous growth and spread of trees alongside the line, this view is no longer a viable proposition. *Ben Ashworth*

Opposite top: On the ground, between thunderstorm and heavy showers, a 'driver's eye view' of the viaduct is snapped on 15 June 2009. Retaining the old down-line alignment, the former up side is now taken by grass and the electric cabinet controlling the impulses to operate the delightfully attractive semaphore signal … a long step from wires and pulleys! Note the 15 mph restriction for the viaduct; and the trees to the right hiding the previous view of Bridgnorth. *MJS*

Opposite bottom left: With the Castle ramparts on the left-hand horizon, we have moved from the viaduct and approach Bridgnorth. This view from 27 March 1966 once again highlights the switchback nature of the countryside, with the valley of the River Severn, on the right, about to course through the lower part of the town.

Opposite bottom right: The Castle rock is still just visible on 15 June 2009, despite the efforts of the trees to mask it, but to the right the valley floor is now completely hidden from view by the magnitude of arboreal growth. On the distant bend the parapets of the bridge over town's bypass are now in place and, alongside the track, telegraph poles have sprouted. *D. Bott/MJS*

The aforementioned bypass, the A458 route to Much Wenlock from the town, was much needed to help alleviate the disastrous level of road congestion at this popular tourist spot. Built in 1982/3, it has served its purpose, but such is the constant expansion of road traffic that the town is still a nightmare through which to drive! On 6 November 1982, in this view from the south during the first week of operations, the final approach to Bridgnorth is temporarily breached by construction work. The semaphores will have to wait for their next trains!

From that gantry, looking south on the same day, the works are seen from a higher elevation, showing the route being carved on the approaches to the railway, with the River Severn sweeping close by. It is to be hoped that the 'Stop' sign on the track panel was never needed! *Both Hugh Ballantyne*

A second road bridge, over the B4363 to Oldbury, quickly follows the bypass and creates the limit to the station confines. On 17 April 1993 No 6960 *Raveningham Hall* accelerates towards this bridge as the 1250 departure for Kidderminster. To the left stand the railway's mobile crane and a Class 25, and to the right of the track a sign spells out the private nature of the site. Built in 1944 at Swindon Works, the second of Hawksworth's 'Modified Halls', No 6960 spent much of its life at Old Oak Common and Reading before a move to Oxford on 31 August 1963 and

withdrawal 12 months later. A quick dispatch to Barry saw it in the sea air on the Docks for eight years, before rescue in 1972. It was returned to steam in 1975.

By 15 June 2009 the previous view across to the town is denied us, but the telegraph pole and SVR warning sign are still in situ, the latter showing the ravages of time! To the left, the crane is still in the siding, although in a marginally different position, as No 7714 leaves the station with the 1350 roster to Kidderminster. *Tom Heavyside/MJS*

Main picture: **Sixteen miles from Kidderminster the rails approach Bridgnorth station. When photographed on 27 March 1966 there was an air of abandonment, the passenger services having been withdrawn from 9 September 1963 and full closure coming on the following 2 December. The siding to the right has been long unused and those into the former goods yard on the left have either been lifted or are smothered by grass. The buildings stand intact, as if employees were about to return.**

Inset above: **The same vantage point on 15 June 2009 is deceptive. The main station building and footbridge are unchanged, but to the left the yard has been transformed by the creation of a four-road engine shed, while to the right the platform has been extended to cope with the longer trains now run by the SVR. The siding now contains coaching stock, and elsewhere the area has been 'tarted up' by paint, seating and flowerbeds.** *D. Bott/MJS*

Inset right top: **Immediately to the west of the line, at the southern end of Bridgnorth station, is the intriguingly named Pan Pudding Hill, an ancient Roman fortification. Viewed from that vantage point, class leader No 82000 pauses in the pouring rain of 22 September 1958, operating as the popular 1.45pm Shrewsbury-Kidderminster service. The goods yard on the left is being well used and the whole scene looks healthy, despite the weather! Like others of the class already seen, this 'Standard 3' was new in 1952, and like those early class members Tyseley was to be its first home, with several transfers thereafter. The majority of its very short life of a little over 14 years was spent in the West Midlands and Wales, before a move to Patricroft (in the Midland Region) in April 1965. Its demise came on the last day of 1966.**

Inset right: **A decade later and the operator is now private, BR having closed the line in 1963. On 13 April 1968 No 3205 is seen again, this time leaving with a special enthusiasts' train bound for Hampton Loade. The Severn Valley Railway Society began in 1965 and undertook weed-clearing tasks at the site, even though it was still owned by BR. Narrowly thwarting attempts by BR to lift the track, the first items of rolling stock arrived in 1967, but public services did not start until 1970, hence the presence of so many supporters on this special day two years earlier.**
H. C. Casserley/Ben Ashworth

Left: The view from the foot of Pan Pudding Hill on 22 March 1958 portrays a further 'Standard 3', No 82007, wreathed in steam as it departs with another Shrewsbury-Kidderminster working comprising the de rigueur three coaches. This was another well-travelled engine, to a wide number and variety of sheds, before finally settling at Bristol (Barrow Road) for just 18 months from November 1962 until the end in July 1964 and scrapping in February 1966.

Lower left: Time has moved on but the motive power has gone back! On 30 August 1962 the more ancient ex-GWR No 4114 pauses for water, with the fireman atop the tank, before leaving for the south with a very mixed rake of freight vehicles, after shunting in the station yard and demonstrating that the level of freight was not insubstantial even at this late date. Apart from a move to Penzance for just one month, and stays at Worcester and Severn Tunnel Junction, the tank spent its allocated life at Kidderminster shed, its home when seen here. Sadly, it did not survive until the closure of that shed, its withdrawal being on 30 November 1963.

Opposite: Forty-seven years later there has been change and no change! The station building and footbridge are as they were, apart from refreshed paintwork and the hanging of platform numbers from the bridge, and the trackwork is basically unaltered, but there has been more dramatic change on the far platform, which has been lengthened to handle the much longer trains needed to accommodate the large numbers of passengers now visiting the railway. Seating and flower baskets also aid the general ambience of the site to a beneficial effect as seen on 15 June 2009. *Gerald Adams, MJS collection/Michael Mensing/MJS*

Opposite top: The fascinating story of the salvation of No 45110 from the cutter's torch, after the end of steam on BR in 1968, is well told by its saviour, David Porter, in Silver Link's book *The Last Years of British Rail 1965-68*. That story also explains why the loco was later named *RAF Biggin Hill*. The naming ceremony took place on the SVR on 12 September 1971, and the loco is seen leaving Bridgnorth station on that day with the 1259 nine-coach train to Hampton Loade, proudly wearing its brand new identity. An RAF Guard of Honour stands to attention as the train leaves, with a corps of trumpeters on the bridge at ease, having played their part. *D. C. Williams, MJS collection*

Above: Steam locomotives by their very nature are thirsty beasts! Depending on their tank/tender capacity they often had to break their journey to take water, with smaller engines saddled by this disadvantage to a greater degree. On 14 September 1956 No 4641 pauses at Bridgnorth to fill its tanks while operating the 4.20pm Shrewsbury-Kidderminster turn, with the fireman on high watching the levels and his driver overseeing from the platform. A lady with her young charge in his pram watch the procedure.

Opposite top: We have already just seen No 82007, but it is here captured a few moments earlier on 22 March 1958. The crew prepare to refill their charge but something must have intervened, as the 'bag' has been placed in the mouth of the tank but is still limp and both crew members are on the platform. Note the '84G' and 'SC' plates on the

smokebox door, denoting an allocation to Shrewsbury – it left there and the line three months later – and a self-cleaning smokebox. A northbound freight passes on the adjacent line.

Opposite: By 3 April 1982 the operation is much the same, but now in private hands as No 5164 receives attention before moving to the head of the coaching stock on the left and proceeding south to Bewdley. Apart from the SVR now being in control, other changes are the more prosaic design of water column and pipe, compared to the 'swan neck' as seen earlier; also the extension to the platform can clearly be seen, the larger edging slabs beginning level with the loco's buffer beam. Young and old crowd on the platform and footbridge to 'relive the dream'! *Richard Casserley/Gerald Adams, MJS collection/Tom Heavyside*

Left: Another view of water being taken, but this time from the footbridge: on a dull 18 August 1962 No 3788 is on the receiving end, at precisely 2.53pm, as No W32W arrives from the south. Allocated to Worcester for many years, the Railcar was sent to South Wales after being discarded by BR, to be scrapped by Birds Commercial Motors Ltd, Risca, in January 1965. By comparison, No 3788 was a long-lived loco. Shedded at Shrewsbury from before 1948 until November 1964, it decamped to Stourbridge Junction then, just one month later, to Oxley, on the outskirts of Wolverhampton. That sojourn was also short, however, with its end coming on 7 October 1965. It, too, went to a Birds Commercial Motors Ltd site, but this time at Long Marston, in January 1966.

Main picture: At the same spot as No 3788, but travelling in the opposite direction, No 7802 *Bradley Manor* arrives at Bridgnorth on 15 June 2009 with the 1025 train from Kidderminster. The lamp post regnant left of centre in the earlier view is still in situ, but now without its lamp-bearing arm, the newer water column and catcher beyond are

in the same positions as their predecessors, and the platform starter signal is as before, but the lengthened platform can again be seen and a new signal gantry has appeared above the loco. Pan Pudding Hill, to the right, looks much as it has done for decades. *Edwin Wilmshurst/MJS*

Top: We have already seen No 45110 moments after being named, but here it is two months earlier, bringing empty stock into Platform 2 on 3 July 1971. In its more anonymous persona it was still a celebrity, being the last steam locomotive to haul a rostered passenger working on BR, on 11 August 1968. With Railcar and coaching stock to the right and engines in the shed yard to the left, there is plenty for the visitors to see and enjoy.

Above: The same view approaching four decades later sees a rather more diminutive engine on duty. Ex-GWR saddle tank No 813 (Port Talbot Railway No 26) is the sole survivor of a class of six built by Hudswell Clarke in 1901 and inherited by the GWR at the Grouping of 1923. Sold by that railway in 1934 to the coal industry, it is a remarkable survivor, having been purchased from the National Coal Board in 1967 and moved in the same year from Backworth Colliery, Northumberland, to the SVR, where the lengthy task of restoration was subsequently undertaken. On 19 September 2008 it returned to its nominal home on the SVR for a short period and was here giving shuttles between Bridgnorth and Highley (denoted by the 'HL' code on the buffer). *Tom Heavyside/MJS*

Left: The beauty of high summer is the ability to photograph later into the evening, when the light is superb for creating long shadows and picking out details. Although not in pristine external condition, the station still makes an attractive tableau as it stands in the evening light of 21 July 1963. The platform and station buildings including the full length of the signalbox look well cared for despite the proximity to closure.

Below: Exactly 46 years have passed, but the view is now looking to the south. The signal box is now in its truncated form. Before the preservationists could stop things, demolition had begun on the box, but they managed to prevent too much desolation and have rebuilt it to three-quarter length – note that there are only three window bays instead of four, No 7714 slows for the termination of the 1210 from Kidderminster, with the driver seemingly not welcoming his portrait being taken, judging by his expression! *Richard Casserley/MJS*

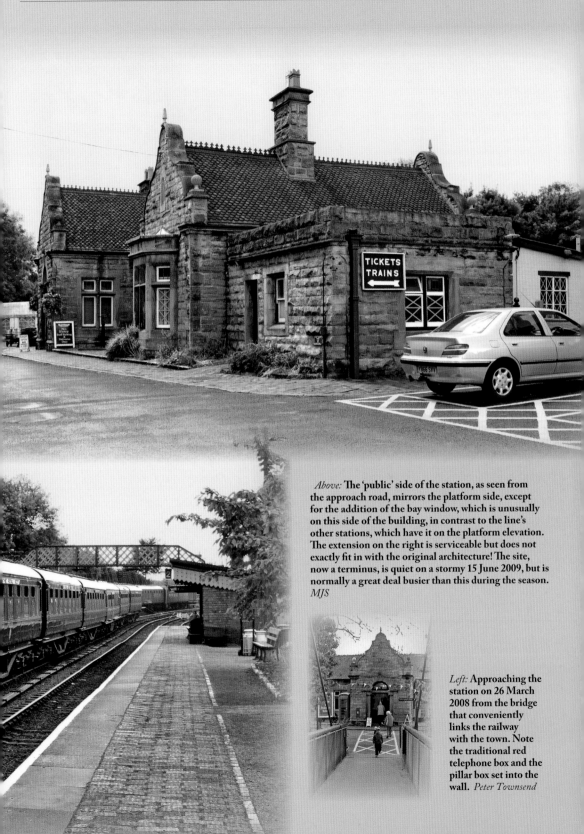

Above: The 'public' side of the station, as seen from the approach road, mirrors the platform side, except for the addition of the bay window, which is unusually on this side of the building, in contrast to the line's other stations, which have it on the platform elevation. The extension on the right is serviceable but does not exactly fit in with the original architecture! The site, now a terminus, is quiet on a stormy 15 June 2009, but is normally a great deal busier than this during the season. *MJS*

Left: Approaching the station on 26 March 2008 from the bridge that conveniently links the railway with the town. Note the traditional red telephone box and the pillar box set into the wall. *Peter Townsend*

Below: As the nascent SVR developed and more locomotives began arriving, all parts of the site were put to use. In this view from 22 May 1971 the siding around the flank of the stone goods shed is home to Nos 70000 *Britannia* and 80079, as an industrial saddle tank busies itself in the background alongside the cream-coloured Exeter building. Twenty years old at this date, having been the first of the new 'Standards' to appear, in January 1951, withdrawal for *Britannia* came on 16 July 1966 from Newton Heath shed. Initially saved for and by the NRM in York, ownership was later transferred to a private company, but it would take until 1991 before it was restored to steam and run on the main line. Note that it still wears its white cab roof, a memento of pulling King George VI's funeral train in 1952. By contrast, No 80079 was notable as being the first of the class to be fitted with plain-section coupling rods, rather than the fluted type that graced its predecessors and had caused problems.

Left: Barely recognisable as the same location, the access path and gateposts in the foreground are an immediate link, together with the sloping roof of the old goods shed just visible through the leaves, upper right. No business can stand still and, certainly, the SVR has made great strides over the past 40 years, with new ideas and buildings to cope being developed over the years. The space once taken by No 80079 is now subsumed within the engine shed extension. *Colour-Rail.com/MJS*

Above: The siding housing *Britannia* on the previous page connected with the main running line to the north of the goods shed, and by 1972 was protected by gates. These are seen barring entrance to ex-LMS 8F No 8233 on a bitterly cold day in October of that year. The loco is not in active service, as can be judged by the shield across the chimney top. The Exeter building stands to the right, as a visitor huddles against the cold in her white fur coat!

Below: Again the vista has changed, but there are pointers to the accuracy of the location on 15 June 2009: the building on the hill and the tracks to the right, the alignment of the siding holding the bogie bolster wagon, but now truncated, and the distant concrete post to the left of No 8233 in 1972. The latter is now by the far end of the wagon, just visible beyond the roof of the car, above the driver's position. The curve to the buffer stop, just short of the tunnel, can be seen in the distance in both views. *Both MJS*

Right: Established as the engineering centre of the new railway, the old goods area alongside the station became the site for the engine shed. Initially this meant locos stored in the open, with just limited facilities in the old goods shed for some of the work to be undertaken. This view on 20 May 1973 exemplifies the open nature of the site at that time, as ex-LMS 8F No 8233 is coaled by the mobile crane, 'Jinty' No 47383 is stripped for overhaul in the foreground, and No 3205 waits a call to arms in the background. The trio of smaller buildings are all remnants of the previous BR presence.

Below: As can be seen, 21 March 1996 was an eventful day. The steam on No 2 road is from ex-GWR 'Heavy Goods' No 4277, then owned by Peter Best and just about to move under its own steam for the first time since rescue from scrapping. With the two buildings in the main yard having been removed and a new purpose-built shed provided to give cover to some of the allocation, it begins to look more like the 'real thing'. Elsewhere in the yard are Nos 47383 (again), 4566, 80079 and '08' shunter D3586. The shed building was fitted with roller-shutter doors in May 2009. *Tom Heavyside/MJS*

Chapter 5
Bridgnorth to Ironbridge

To finish our look at the operational areas of Bridgnorth, we are transported back to the so-called 'good old days', when steam still ruled. Viewed from the northern end of the down platform at Bridgnorth on 30 March 1955, No 8718 slowly pushes its mixed consist of cattle truck, box vans and sundry other types away from the station, with the back end snaking onto the adjacent running line. The town, 18 miles from Hartlebury, the official starting point of the branch, can clearly be seen from this angle, High Town perched high above the lower half and the River Severn and railway. As seen earlier, No 8718 was a long-term resident of Kidderminster shed and duly wears the relevant '85D' shedplate in this view. The shunter stands with his pole in the 'four foot' on the left, waiting for his next task. *Gerald Adams, MJS collection*

Above: When the railway north of Bridgnorth was proposed, there were two basic options: to tunnel under High Town, the medieval heart of the area, or to cross over the Severn to the lower ground to the east. The latter would have taken the railway away from the population, so the 550-yard tunnel was built. Emerging on 30 August 1962, 12 months from closure, No 80079 heads for Shrewsbury with the 7.27pm train from Bridgnorth – a completely empty train, despite the town having the largest population along the branch! Note the chimneys of two of the many industrial sites alongside the Severn, and the tower of St Mary's Church on the extreme right.

Below: There have been calls to rebuild the 8 miles of railway to connect with Ironbridge, but apart from a potentially high price to reopen the tunnel for rail traffic, the trackbed is no longer available. The lady on the right is climbing from a small park that incorporates the trackbed, designated by the trees in the centre of the picture and the adjacent house. The tunnel mouth is some 100 yards to the right of this 21 June 2009 view. *Michael Mensing/MJS*

Main picture: A little further along the line from Bridgnorth, the two chimneys are again seen, together with a gasholder, apparently nearly full, and, again, to the extreme right, the tower of Telford-designed St Mary's Church. With its light load of just two coaches, the previously seen 7.27pm to Shrewsbury on Saturday 8 June 1963 enjoys the lowering evening sun, with No 41209 not having to exert any great effort.

Inset: There is yet more evidence on 21 June 2009 as to why there could be no reinstatement of the railway at this point. The houses mirror the route of the branch and, with the obliteration of any semblance of a railway here, one wonders how many of the residents are aware of the heritage of their property. *Michael Mensing/MJS*

Right: A mile or so north of Bridgnorth, with the railway sitting slightly above the meadowland leading to the Severn, No 4129 crosses the end of a narrow lane on 30 August 1962 with a rake of loaded coal wagons bound for Ironbridge Power Station. Across the river Fort Pendlestone dominates its surroundings; a long-time landmark of this stretch of the Severn – and not immune from flooding – this historic sandstone building has been converted over the years into business units and, more recently, apartments with fishing rights and views over the River Severn towards Bridgnorth Golf Club. Note the well-tended allotments in the left foreground. *Michael Mensing*

Far left: Four miles from Bridgnorth, along the valley floor parallel with the river, Linley station was something of an anachronism. With absolutely no indigenous habitation to hand and no road access in any case, it was built entirely at the behest – and at the great cost – of Thomas Whitmore of nearby Apley Park, which was also well away from public roads. Situated on the other side of the river and only connected by means of a suspension bridge, he nevertheless demanded that the station have at least two trains each way per day that he could stop by request! In this view from 1962, looking towards Shrewsbury, there was once a siding to the left of the station building, but that had closed seven years beforehand. The isolated nature is obvious in this portrait.

Left: Despite – or because of? – the apparent isolation, Station House has remained occupied after closure; indeed, with the scaffolding seeming to indicate renovation, it would appear to have a future. The platform was inaccessible when visited on 21 June 2009, but had been recently cleared of vegetation and the edging is clearly visible, with the erstwhile trackbed to its right. Other than the disappearance of a chimney on the low building, the rest is as before, including the retention of the corrugated-iron hut. *Great Western Trust collection/MJS*

Above: Moving to the northern end of the platform and looking back towards Bridgnorth on 31 August 1963, a week from closure, a DMU pauses at the station with the 3.02pm departure for Shrewsbury. Apart from the young lady on the platform end, the station could almost have been a *Marie Celeste*! Note the bike temporarily abandoned in the bushes on the left. The reduction of staffing and some services led to the station being renamed Linley Halt on 10 September 1951.

Below: With the railway gone, the trackbed is now open to walkers, cyclists and even the occasional car, to Station House and a handful of houses and a fishing club a few hundred yards towards Bridgnorth. By 21 June 2009 the canopy and seating have gone from the former waiting room, together with the lamp from the platform, but otherwise the fine design has been left largely unaltered, though now surrounded by trees, rather than the previously more open aspect. *David Johnson/MJS*

Main picture: Three miles further on, Coalport was one of two stations to grace the eponymous settlement. Unfortunately, although the Severn Valley facility was on a through route – from somewhere to somewhere – it was sited on the wrong side of the river for the village, which was accessed by a bridge some distance below the station site. With the LNWR branch from Wellington as competition, it was therefore less able than might otherwise have been the case to bolster the line's receipts, and trains such as the one seen here would have served relatively few travellers. Indeed, it was the last station on the route to be modernised, not being provided with a second platform and passing loop until 1895. On an unidentified date in the early 1950s, Worcester-based No 4139 pauses with a Worcester-Shrewsbury train – the loco moved away, to Bristol, on 21 February 1953.

Note the unusual advertising on the main building – 'Astons for Furniture … Baby Cars … Furniture … Bedding'!

Above right: Once again the station building is in private hands and, indeed, the site is home to both people and a small business, 'Coalport Station Holidays', which offers self-catering holiday lets in the two coaches

seen at the far end of the right-hand platform – a sort of homage to GWR Camping Coaches! On 21 June 2009 the buildings and both platforms are much as they were, with the disappearance of the toilet block making room for more parking and a gap in the up platform to allow access. *MJS collection/MJS, with permission*

Climbing the steep road to the road overbridge, the station site is seen in wider view, including the half-mile siding in the distance, busy with a loco shunting rakes of wagons. On 7 April 1960 Railcar No W32W draws to a halt to allow the handful of travellers to board. Compared to the previous decade, the station garden on the left has been carefully tended; the advertising has been removed from the toilet block; the lamps have been dispensed with on the up platform; and a TV aerial has appeared on the main chimney. A Worcester resident for much of its later life, No W32W was to end its days at Birds Commercial Motors Ltd, Risca, being cut there in January 1965.

One of the photographer's enemies, the explosion of foliage, has again prevented an exact copy, so the 'present' view is slightly to the left of the earlier one. The two coaches are seen more clearly; the distant trackbed is now a road; lamps have returned to the platform; the station garden is making a comeback on the left; and, despite the driving rain on 21 June 2009, the site is obviously being cared for. *RAS, MJS collection/MJS*

Turning round and looking towards Shrewsbury, No W32W is again seen on its travels on 7 April 1960. The pointwork for the loop in Coalport station is in the right foreground and the distant semaphore and the 40 mph speed restriction sign protect the approach. Note the proximity of the River Severn to the line, in the left distance, and yet more factories on its banks. Not only is this an historic industrial heartland, but its also remains very attractive countryside. *RAS, MJS collection*

Here is a very rare colour view of Jackfield Halt, taken from a train on a dull 5 August 1963. Despite having a population of more than 1,000 at the dawn of the 20th century, and its ceramic tile factories being world-renowned and flourishing, the village was not furnished with a station until 3 December 1934. A very basic affair, it was adjacent to the level crossing for the road that originally led to the village, nestled on the banks of the Severn. In the spring of 1952 a major landslip caused the railway and the Halt to move 25 feet down the slope towards the river! The station was moved a quarter of a mile further east, opening on 1 March 1954, but gangers were on constant duty, realigning and reballasting the track, and by the late 1950s most of the centre of the village, an area called Salthouses, had been demolished. A 5 mph speed restriction was placed on the railway over the site. A combination of progressive mining and the Doughty Fault led to a further landslip in the 1980s – and again early in this century – destroying the road that had been built to replace that lost in the 1950s. The area is still unstable and the ground is continually moving, to the effect that the 'new' road, built on the trackbed after the closure of the railway, is akin to a massive switchback and is in need of constant attention. The history of the area is fascinating and repays diligent research. *Barry Hilton*

Above: The erstwhile trackbed continues to move and the previous alignment is in flux. This view from 21 June 2009 is close to the 1954 site seen in 1962, but not part of the new road, and the post on the extreme left confirms it by announcing the 'Severn Valley Way'. Maws factory, once the largest tile manufacturer in the world, with product seen in the Houses of Westminster and the like, is now residential flats and is hidden by the trees to the left. *MJS*

Above: Here is another view of the Halt in 1962, looking towards Shrewsbury, with some of the many old works in the background. The building was moved bodily from the original site and is as seen earlier, with the exception of the absence of two supporting wooden pillars for the canopy, which also held the station nameboard. *Great Western Trust collection*

Main picture: I make no apologies for repeating this image from the first volume, for not only is it a pleasing view of a train leaving the station, but it also depicts the cramped site, with the road wall on the extreme left and sidings on both sides of the running lines, and how close the location was to the bridge – it deserves a larger space to do it justice. On Easter Monday, 30 March 1959, No 82008 leads its short rake of two Western coaches away from Ironbridge & Broseley station as the 1.45pm Shrewsbury-Bewdley service. The depth and steepness of the Gorge can be well judged, on both sides of the river, with the bridge forming the link. *Michael Mensing*

Above: A rare sight: the renowned H. C. Casserley in front of the camera for a change! Captured by his son, he stands before the wooden goods shed on 17 April 1959, when the route was still in full operation. Geographic constraints dictated that the railway be built on the south of the river, which not only meant great expense for the railway, to create an embankment and plateau supported by a massive 15-metre retaining wall, but also that potential passengers from Ironbridge itself had to pay a toll to cross the bridge to reach the railway – not the most encouraging of situations! Although tolls were abolished in 1950, it was then too late to recover lost trade, with the growth of motor traffic.

Right: Standing now on the down platform on the same day, we have a closer view of the station buildings. Note the separation of 'Iron' and 'Bridge' on the sign board; the

crossing gates protecting the road access to a former brick and tile works; the brick-built footbridge beyond; the loss of the original waiting shelter on the left-hand platform, together with the semaphores controlling the rail approach to the crossing; and the disappearance of the signal box on the far side of the crossing. In contrast, a new goods shed has been inserted alongside the 'Gents'.

Left: It is hardly believable that this is the same site 50 years on, but the building to the right of the station above is still extant. The former trackbed is now basically the entrance road to the various parts of the car park, which, as viewed on 21 June 2009, is extremely popular with visitors, especially at the very reasonable rates. *Richard Casserley/H. C. Casserley/MJS*

Above: **Admittedly this is a somewhat depressing view across the Gorge from the station on 14 September 1956, but it shows the crowded and ancient nature of the buildings on the town side, together with the narrow strip between platform and retaining wall, containing a grounded vintage carriage, and a very small and insignificant station sign!**

Below: **Although the bridge has now become virtually invisible, due to the clamour of the trees for upward growth, many of the houses across the Gorge are still clearly seen and still in place, with one or two newer ones now interspersed. Taking a slightly wider angle, the retaining wall remains intact on 21 June 2009, but the public is now discouraged from venturing towards it by much sturdier fencing than of yore.** *Richard Casserley/MJS*

Above: As if echoing the sadness of our photographer at having to leave the station, the rain beats down on the scene on 22 September 1958, as the train prepares to restart its southward journey. A box van stands on the dead-end siding through the goods shed and, beyond, the road climbs and curves on its way to Broseley. Note the long expanse of footbridge, spanning the running line and the adjacent road.

Below: Five decades later, that road still curves sharply upwards – though not now in the rain! – and the inherent tree line is as before, but now with greater height! The house to the left stands in clear view, rather than the glimpse of the gable roof beyond the goods shed in 1956. On 21 June 2009 all bays at this end of the car park are full. *H. C. Casserley/MJS*

Our final view of Ironbridge & Broseley is from that long footbridge, looking back along the line towards Bridgnorth. On an unidentified date No 5153 appears to be running wrong line as it heads for Ironbridge Power Station with its rake of loaded coal wagons, watched by a staff member – but no doubt it has a clear run onto the single track shortly after leaving the station and will, therefore, not need to avoid any due passenger trains. Seemingly devoid of shedplate, it has probably only recently undertaken its transfer from Newton Abbot, which took effect on 8 September 1962, when it moved to Kidderminster. Thus it is within the final year of operations on the line. *Great Western Trust collection*

Left: Such has been the obliteration of the station site at Buildwas Junction, with no meaningful landmarks/points of comparison now available, that the views here are all from the past, to show just what has been lost. Only a mile from Ironbridge, the terrain was vastly different, with substantial areas of flat land! On 22 September 1958, this is the view towards Ironbridge as our photographer's train leaves for the south, with the lines from Much Wenlock coming in from the right. *H. C. Casserley*

Chapter 5
Buildwas to Shrewsbury

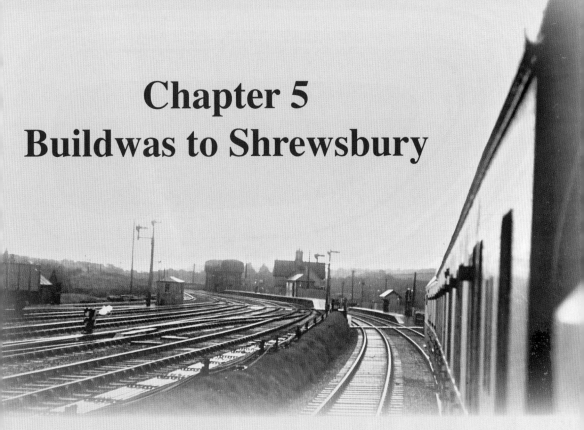

Above: **Looking back from that same train, the Severn Valley platforms stand at a lower level than the single one for Much Wenlock. The myriad of lines on the left also includes the branch coming in from Coalbrookdale, by way of an underpass to the Severn Valley line.** *H. C. Casserley*

Main picture: **A few yards outside of the station, on our journey from the south, the difference in elevation of the two sides of the station can be seen much more clearly. To the left, No 9639 waits to leave with the 11.40am Much Wenlock-Wellington local service on 17 April 1959. Note that the three platforms are joined by steps and a boarded crossing, and that the station architecture mirrors that further down the line.** *H. C. Casserley*

Above: Greek meets Greek! Moving to the up platform, a 'Mickey Mouse' drifts into the station on 5 August 1963, on its way south, to be met by one its fellow class members, whose crew pose for their portraits before leaving for Shrewsbury. *Barry Hilton*

Top right: Looking south, we again see the 11.40am for Much Wenlock behind No 9639. The large running-in sign reads 'Change here for Much Wenlock and Wellington lines', but until 31 December 1951 'Craven Arms' had also been part of the sign, in the days when the service ran beyond Much Wenlock to that location. *H. C. Casserley*

Main picture: Looking south moments before the middle view on the previous page, No 41209 seems to be champing at the bit, raring to be on its way to Shrewsbury. As we have seen from previous views, this was a popular engine for the services close to the final days, and this view, from 5 August 1963, is just a month away from the end. *Barry Hilton*

Above: Crossing to the down platform, an unidentified 'Standard 3' pauses in the bright sunshine of 9 June 1959. Its crew take time out to enjoy the warm sunshine and the peace of this isolated station, before continuing their journey to Shrewsbury. In many ways, Buildwas was akin to Trent Junction, on the London Midland Region, being a busy exchange/meeting point of various lines but away from any community and with no easy access other than by rail. *Great Western Trust collection*

Opposite top: Four miles from Buildwas and just 8 miles from Shrewsbury, Cressage station was opened in 1862, on the north-western edge of the community close to the crossroads in the centre of the village. Initially with just a single platform, the loop, signal box and second platform were introduced in 1894. In this view 65 years later, on 10 June 1959, little of importance has changed, with the four crossing gates still in position, protecting the B4380 road and controlled by wheel from the signal box that can just be seen at the end of the down platform. *Great Western Trust collection*

Right: A comparative view in the 21st century is prevented by tall hedges, an extension to the station building encroaching onto the old platform area, and landscaping of the erstwhile trackbed, so we look back from a train about to cross the road on 22 September 1958. The small waiting shelter, substantially built for a relatively out-of-the-way station, was part of the additions of June 1894. Housing now obliterates the far side of the crossing, behind the photographer in this view. *H. C. Casserley*

Right: Another view from 10 June 1959 sees yet another 'Standard 3', No 82004, about to leave Cressage for the journey south with its three-coach train from Shrewsbury. The proximity of the road, crossing signal box, station buildings and, on the right, a tiny station garden, together with a boarded foot crossing, are all well displayed from this vantage point. As seen earlier, this still relatively young locomotive was reduced to scrap metal in February 1966.

Above: The same view 50 years later, on 21 June 2009, shows the extent of the aforementioned landscaping. In essence, the station building is little changed on this elevation, the fitting of a newer window being the only really noticeable difference. Surrounded by tall trees and hedges, the location is a peaceful haven, enjoyed by its residents. *Great Western Trust collection/MJS, with permission*

Below: Stepping over the crossing, our final look more clearly shows the signal box, with the signalman posing for his portrait on 10 June 1959. The four-gate arrangement is also shown, together with the Stop signal at the platform's end. *Great Western Trust collection*

Opposite top left: While most photographs in the 'Past and Present' series portray trains and/or stations, our photographer has here rung the changes and given us an unusual view of an entrance to a station. On 17 April 1959 he has temporarily halted his tour of the Severn Valley line to look at Cound Halt and give us this road scene, including the diminutive sign announcing the location! Note that his well-travelled car is the only one bringing passengers here on this day.

Opposite centre left: Approximately a mile and a half from Cressage, along the busy A458 road, the station site is adjacent to yet another ferry crossing of the Severn and, as such, is a favourite stopping place for visitors who can then enjoy a drink and/or meal at the hostelry hidden behind the trees on the left. The old wall is still in place, but has now been extended at a slight angle, to finish roughly where the car is above, to move access to the crest of the rise. On 21 June 2009 the pub had a healthy number of patrons. *H. C. Casserley/MJS*

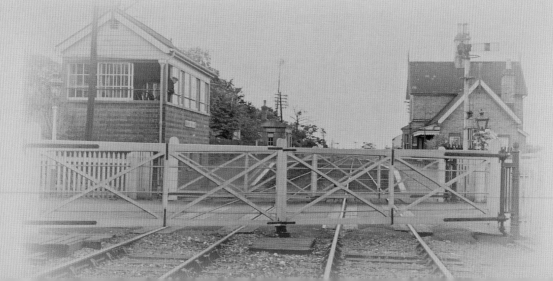

Top right: The actual entrance path to the station was similarly limited in its designation, with just the small 'GWR To Cound Halt' notice on the telegraph pole. The River Severn can be seen through the open gateway on 17 April 1959, and also attached to the pole is a reference to the Cound Lodge Inn having fishing rights over the waters, with permits available at 2/-!

Centre right: Stepping back slightly, the old access is now more open but still as steep as ever. The river is again clearly seen, with its sharp, almost-90-degree, bend to the right passing beyond the parked cars. A private fishing notice is displayed, but not so prominently on 21 June 2009.
H. C. Casserley/MJS

Despite the best efforts of your author and helpful cooperation on the ground, a comparative shot was just

impossible, due to fencing, overgrowth of the trackbed, etc. This then was the structure on 17 April 1959 that awaited the intrepid traveller. Not opened until 4 August 1934, during the major campaign by the GWR to open lineside Halts in an attempt to drum up trade, it was virtually identical to Jackfield Halt, but was seemingly more useful to fishermen than to the residents of Cound, some distance away. It remained open, as a request stop, until closure of the line in 1963. Note the steps down to the river, just visible centre left; and the Cound Lodge Inn in the background.

The view towards Shrewsbury, at around the same period, amply demonstrates the 'cheap' nature of these Halts. Though neat and tidy, being built entirely of wood, with the GWR obviously trying to restrain the budget as much as possible, it is unlikely that this location ever really repaid the investment. *Richard Casserley/Great Western Trust collection*

Above: **Berrington was a further 2½ miles towards Shrewsbury along the A458. The first station out of Shrewsbury on the line, with the village close by, it was a relatively important station, with just short of 17,000 tickets being issued in 1903, some no doubt connected with the nearby Cross Houses Union Workhouse, later a hospital. Again opened as a single platform, 1894 saw the loop and second platform provided, as well as the doubling of the low waiting room, to give accommodation to waiting ladies. During a wet spell on the visit of 17 April 1959, the attendant signal box and small shelter on the down platform can be glimpsed beyond, but partly hidden by, the semaphore.**

Below: **Happily, on many occasions the residents of previous station buildings are predisposed to retain as many features as possible, and those at Berrington over the years have been no exception. When viewed from the nearby road bridge on 21 June 2009, both the property and its surroundings look in tremendous condition, with the trackbed grassed over and kept in good trim, right on into the distance, with the alignment that took a siding to a weighbridge behind the main building. On the down platform, the former small waiting shelter has been replaced by a simple covered structure; the up platform has a new shed and a partition erected between the old waiting rooms and the main structure; the waiting rooms have had an upper window fitted; and there is now a bridge between the two platforms.** *Richard Casserley/MJS*

Above: We are now on the south-western outskirts of Shrewsbury, not far from the point where the Severn Valley line was crossed by that into the old Abbey station. On Saturday 24 September 1960 No 4178 climbs away from Sutton Bridge Junction with its three coaches, forming the 1.45pm Shrewsbury-Hartlebury service. New out of Swindon Works on 29 November 1949, under the aegis of British Railways but to the GWR design, its first home was Carmarthen in deepest south-west Wales. A much-travelled loco thereafter, it was at this time nominally shedded in Exeter, but was due to transfer to Wellington; no doubt the latter had acquired its new arrival early and had immediately put it to work! Painted in black lined livery when new, it here wears an attractive lined green coat. It had the honour of hauling the last train on the Much Wenlock branch on 21 July 1962, the 7.05pm to Wellington. Withdrawal was from Oxley on 9 October 1965, with cutting coming soon after, at Birds Commercial Motors Ltd, Long Marston, in February 1966.

Below: In 1960 No 4178 was passing through an oasis of green amidst the ever-spreading tarmac and brick of Shrewsbury, with some elderly housing stock in the background. However, in the 21st century all this has been swallowed by yet more residential development.
Both Michael Mensing

Right: We have now arrived at our destination. 'Standard 5' 4-6-0 No 73090 waits patiently in a bay platform to form the 11.13am stopping service to Stafford in 1965. Yet another locomotive whose time came prematurely, it was new just ten years before this view, on 8 October 1955, but succumbed to the accountants and the inevitable on 31 October 1965. Already here demoted to more minor duties, it had previously worked much longer and arduous tasks, from Patricroft (in Manchester) and Oxley (in Wolverhampton) as well as an earlier stint at Shrewsbury. *MJS collection*

Above: The magnificent Severn Bridge Junction signal box at the south end of Shrewsbury station is now a listed building. Built by the LNWR, it is the largest surviving mechanical signal box in Britain, with a frame of 180 levers, and while the line beyond Abbey Foregate signal box to Wolverhampton has been updated to electronic signalling, Shrewsbury itself is set to remain lever-operated for the foreseeable future. As a result of Shrewsbury's joint (GWR/LNWR) history and subsequent 'musical chairs' between BR Regions, the signalling is a diverse mixture of lower-quadrant and upper-quadrant semaphore signals, with a few colour lights for good measure! With Shrewsbury Abbey behind, the box stands proud on 24 April 1996, with lines crossing in front on the level. *MJS*

Right: Having now completed our journey up the Severn Valley branch, we have exited from the platforms and take a moment to look back at the magnificent frontage of Shrewsbury's station. On 24 April 1996 BR has been 'dead' for two

years, but the yellow van still proudly bears that organisation's logo! The station was originally built in October 1848 for the county's first railway, the Shrewsbury to Chester route, the architect being T. M. Penson. Later augmented in 1901 by the construction of a new floor underneath the original station building, the platforms also extend over the River Severn. Until 1948 it was operated jointly by the GWR and LNWR/LMS. *MJS*

Left: Another broader view on the same day shows unit No 158790 running into the platform with the 1524 'Alphaline' service from Birmingham (New Street). Note the differing types of semaphores and gantries. *MJS*

Right: At its railway height, Shrewsbury was the centre of a web of lines radiating to all points of the compass. As with other such locations throughout the UK, this called for the provision of engine servicing facilities. Being the historical beneficiary of routes operated by the LMS and the GWR, it ended with side-by-side sheds belonging to both. Thus, over time, each side might see locos from the 'opposition', as here, with ex-LMS No 45270 sharing space by the coaling plant with an ex-GWR 'Hall'. Often engines could be seen 'running in' after overhaul from Crewe Works, but a more prosaic duty has brought the 'Black Five' to the shed, during its three-month stay at Chester (6A) shed in 1964. *Nick Lowe, MJS collection*

Below: A year earlier, on 14 July 1963, another LMS type stands with GWR motive power. 'Mickey Mouse' No 46505 is pictured outside the original 1856 Shrewsbury & Hereford Railway (later GWR) brick-built two-road shed, with No 6845 *Paviland Grange* behind. Interestingly, although No 46505 had been an Oswestry resident from new in 1952, and still wears the appropriate (89D) shedplate, it had nominally been transferred away to the other end of the system, at Willesden, four months earlier. Perhaps Willesden was wondering where it was! *MJS*

The BIG Flood of 2007

As mentioned elsewhere within this volume, the SVR was dramatically affected by the severe floods in the summer of 2007. Services over the route were brought to a standstill by a lethal cocktail of flooding and landslides, leading to nearly 50 breaches of the line (see also the comments in the Introduction). The following pages highlight some of the more spectacular locations, but the two shots below depict the twin problems, of the line being swamped or undermined.

Right: **A sign that is both 'past' and 'present'. Taking the lead from the well-known Lord Kitchener poster of the First World War, the SVR made the message loud and clear – 'Your Railway Needs You!'. This cry is not, however, a thing of the past, for either the SVR or any other preserved railway in the UK. All of them need supporters and volunteers, as well as hard cash, and we draw to the end of this book with a reinforcement of the message and an exhortation to anyone reading this to consider whether they too can play a part in the railway's future.** *SVR collection*

Below: **Looking like a miniature 'Mississippi Delta', the effect of the heavy rains is outstanding and very plain to see in this aerial view, out in the countryside. The land has been swept from under the railway, taking soil, rock, ballast and even some trees with it, in the cascade caused by the heavy rains.** *SVR collection*

Right: We will now take a journey northwards from Bewdley to Bridgnorth, stopping off at various points that suffered damage in the floods. First is Northwood Lane, paralleling the railway north from Bewdley, a narrow, twisting, single-track roadway giving sole access to isolated properties along its length. The problems caused by the floods to those residents and others wishing to traverse the route can be judged from this view. Work has already begun in attempting to rectify the situation, with undergrowth on the embankment removed and pinning of the slope begun. Much debris has been cleared from the road, but the conditions are still far from perfect. The railway is atop the escarpment on the left, where a digger is giving assistance.

Main picture: With the undergrowth on the embankment now in rude health, it hardly seems possible that this is the same place but, on 28 July 2009, the scars from two years earlier are but memories. With the tree on the left as the common marker, No 46443 heads north with a train for Bridgnorth. *SVR collection/Dewi Jones*

Top: Situated between Northwood Lane and Victoria Bridge, Folly Point was another location to suffer a severe landslip, with the trackbed, cut into the hillside, being undermined. Once more the remedial works have begun, with stone gabions being put in place to stabilise the land and to give the repaired railway a firm foundation. The narrowness of the alignment at this point can be seen from the approaching rails beyond, and the operator of the road/rail machine must work with great care.

Above: Turning through 180 degrees, No 4566 is seen approaching the location from the south with the 1055 Bridgnorth-Kidderminster service on 28 July 2009, formed of the ex-LNER teak rake. The tiers of gabions, on both sides of the track, are evident, showing just how much work has gone into making the place safe for the passage of trains. Here it is still early days, but nature will eventually colonise the area, softening the stark outline seen in this view. *SVR collection/ Dewi Jones*

Left: North of Folly Point and roughly
halfway along the next stretch of the journey
to Arley station, the railway crosses the
river on the highly attractive and much
photographed Victoria Bridge. The southern
approach is from a cutting, following which

the land drops away and the line traverses the bridge. With the onset of the extraordinary, swift and heavy rainfall in 2007, the dropping away became even more real! As can be seen in this view, looking south towards Bewdley, the gulf that opened up threatened not just the railway but also the piers of the bridge itself. Once more, access was inordinately difficult and much careful thought had to be given to the modus operandi of a successful reinstatement.

Left: Two years later there are no outward signs of any disruption. On 28 July 2009 No 7802 *Bradley Manor* heads north with the 1140 Kidderminster-Bridgnorth turn, with the photographer standing in more of a position of safety than a strict 'past and present' view would dictate! *SVR collection/Dewi Jones*

Right: Fisherman's Crossing is not a widely known location outside the railway but, close to Borle Viaduct on the way north, it is still a vital stretch of the line. These two views show some of the effect of the battering that the area received in June and July 2007, and what damage can be done in such a short time to what is normally regarded as a substantial and 'permanent' way! Faced with such devastation, the track now more resembling a snake than hard steel, together with other similar locations on the railway, it is little short of amazing that not only was the line reopened, but that it was achieved in such a short period as **274 days.** *Both SVR collection*

Above: By far the worst hit, by virtue of the area damaged, was the stretch of line immediately to the south of Highley station. The embankment to the east of the station, between it and the river, was subjected to a massive slippage, with buildings in its wake not escaping the effects. In this view, from that embankment, looking towards the station site, just some of the disruption can be seen.

Below: Once more the skill and determination of the SVR to regain its place within the preservation movement is exemplified in this view from 30 July 2009, when again the ability of man and nature's handiwork have combined to restore the scene to one of seemingly uninterrupted normality. Note the skeleton of the footbridge in place, waiting for the rest to be installed. *SVR collection/Dewi Jones*

Swinging through nearly 180 degrees, this is the view looking south towards Bewdley, with much work already undertaken to remove the unstable parts and rebuild the embankment. As the concrete mixer is on the erstwhile trackbed, one can judge the magnitude of the task in hand to rebuild the railway. The Engine House stands in the background, waiting for normality to return!

Bottom: Again, the combination of man and nature has contrived to repair – and even improve on – the original embankment, seen here on 30 July 2009, with, hopefully, measures now in place to prevent a recurrence of the 2007 problems. Given the thousands of passengers who have been on board trains during the recent past, one wonders how many of them have any idea of the destruction that affected this area. *SVR collection/Dewi Jones*

Left: Oldbury Viaduct, on the final approaches to Bridgnorth, was another structure that was in danger of serious damage, with urgent attention again being needed to shore up the endangered embankment. This view south shows work in progress, with large pipes in place and wooden shuttering ready for concrete pouring.

Right: Moving slightly to the south and turning round to look towards Bridgnorth on a bright and sunny 15 June 2009, the effectiveness of the works is clear, with the viaduct no longer threatened and new electronics in place controlling the semaphore signal. *SVR collection/MJS*

Main picture: **On Tuesday 10 June 2008 the Royal Train visited the SVR, conveying HRH Prince Charles and HRH The Duchess of Cornwall. Arriving after a previous engagement in Worcester, their presence was to see the restored railway, recognise the major efforts to achieve the 'impossible' and to stop at stations on the route to meet many of those involved, including civic leaders, staff and volunteers, and society representatives. No 6024** *King Edward I* **was chosen as the engine to haul the train to Bridgnorth and this view shows it on the outward run.** *SVR collection*

THE ENGINE HOUSE

Built on land adjacent to the station at Highley, The Engine House has been one of the railway's recent major projects. A museum, long desired and the result of many years of planning, fundraising and construction, it provides undercover accommodation for locomotives whose boiler

Main picture: This view, taken on 20 June 2009, is from the track south of Highley station. The old coal sidings, on which the museum sits, have been greatly re-landscaped and the building is most certainly not from the Victorian era! *MJS*

Above left: Travelling back in time, to 29 March 2006, this was the approach road to what would become The Engine House. The adjacent running line can just be glimpsed through the trees to the left, from which the spur to the new museum would travel up through the gates seen here.

Clearance is under way in the middle distance, preparing the site for the contractors, and smoke rises from one of the bonfires.

Above right: By 30 July 2009 the transformation is complete and the further landscaping needed to accommodate the museum building is clear from the comparison of the two views. The rails are in place and now look completely part of the scenery, despite the rather steep gradient up to the building itself. The running line, to the left, is now more easily visible. *David Mee/Dewi Jones*

certificates have expired as well as an education/interpretation centre. Initially, the plan was to open it during 2007, but the intended opening dates were overtaken by the flood damage at Highley station during that summer, with all concentration then placed on actually restoring the operating railway. Rail access to the site, essential for moving locomotives in and out, was finally installed in March 2008. The exhibits were shunted into the building on the 14th and 16th, allowing the museum to open in conjunction with the reopening of the full line. There was a slight hiatus at the beginning of November

2008, when access was not possible by rail as passenger trains did not stop at Highley station while footings and parts of a new footbridge were built. Due to manufacturing problems the completion of the footbridge was deferred until late 2009. Due to be formally opened by Prince Richard, Duke of Gloucester, on 28 April 2009, this had to be postponed to a later date as he was unable to attend due to illness. Algernon Heber-Percy, Lord Lieutenant of Shropshire, deputised in the Prince's absence, to welcome the public, with a formal opening by Prince Richard being scheduled for a later date.

Left: **And so the museum is finally open. With a colliery silver band doing the musical honours, invited guests have their first glimpse of the arrangements, on the ground and from the balcony. Hogging the limelight in this view in the centre background is ex-Longmoor Military Railway 2-10-0 No 600 *Gordon*. Built during the Second World War to a design by the North British Locomotive Co at its Hyde Park Works in Glasgow in 1943, it was the second engine to emerge of a class that eventually numbered 150 engines, and was the last steam locomotive owned by the British Army. Named in honour of the Royal Engineers' most famous General, Charles Gordon ('Gordon of Khartoum'), it was used after the war on the LMR in Hampshire. When that system closed in 1969 it was preserved on the SVR, arriving there in 1972 and operating from the following year. It currently awaits overhaul.**

Alongside on the right is ex-Midland Railway 4-4-0 'Compound' No 1000. Set aside for preservation after withdrawal in 1959 and restored close to its 1914 condition, it is painted in Midland maroon livery. It originally ran enthusiasts' specials before being placed in the temporary Clapham Transport Museum. Though owned by the National Railway Museum in York, it is on long-term loan to the SVR, as a static exhibit in The Engine House. *SVR collection*

End of the day

photo courtesy David Porter